A **FALCON** GUIDE ®

Mountain Biking
Sun Valley, Idaho

Including the Sawtooth Mountains

Greg McRoberts

FALCON GUIDE ®

GUILFORD, CONNECTICUT
HELENA, MONTANA
AN IMPRINT OF THE GLOBE PEQUOT PRESS

*A*FALCONGUIDE®

Library of Congress Cataloging-in-Publication Data is available.
ISBN-13: 978-0-7627-4089-5
ISBN-10: 0-7627-4089-2

Manufactured in the United States of America
First Edition/First Printing

The author and The Globe Pequot Press assume no liability for accidents happening to, or injuries sustained by, readers who engage in the activities described in this book.

This book is dedicated to everyone in the Wood River and Sawtooth Valleys who have contributed their efforts, both physically and financially, to the extensive trail systems we are able to enjoy. This would include the USFS, motorcyclists, private individuals, hikers, equestrians, mountain bikers, the BLM, and countless other (sometimes stealth) individuals. Thank you.

For Quinn

Contents

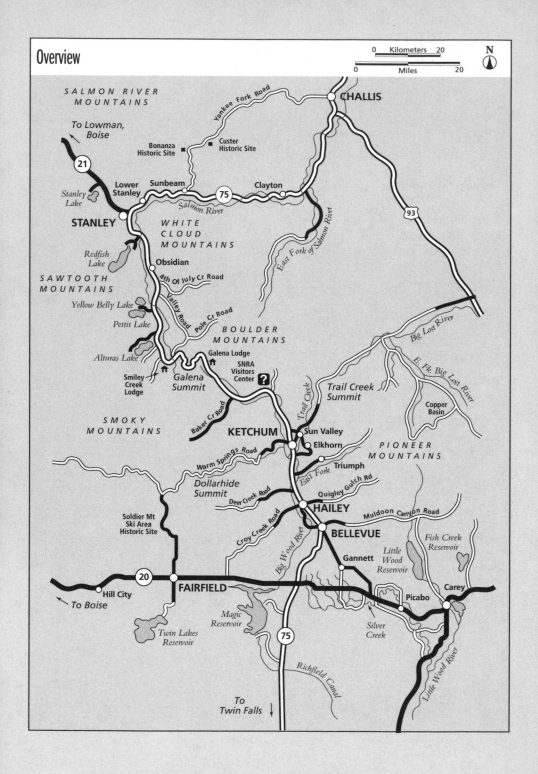

Overview

0 Kilometers 20
0 Miles 20

N

SALMON RIVER MOUNTAINS

To Lowman, Boise

CHALLIS

21

Bonanza Historic Site

Custer Historic Site

Yankee Fork Road

Lower Stanley

Sunbeam

Clayton

75

93

Stanley Lake

Salmon River

STANLEY

WHITE CLOUD MOUNTAINS

East Fork of Salmon River

Redfish Lake

Obsidian

4th Of July Cr Road

SAWTOOTH MOUNTAINS

Yellow Belly Lake

Valley Road

Pole Cr Road

Pettit Lake

BOULDER MOUNTAINS

Big Lost River

Alturas Lake

Galena Lodge

E. Fk. Big Lost River

Smiley Creek Lodge

Galena Summit

SNRA Visitors Center

SMOKY MOUNTAINS

Baker Cr Road

Trail Creek

Trail Creek Summit

Copper Basin

KETCHUM

Sun Valley

PIONEER MOUNTAINS

Warm Springs Road

Elkhorn

Triumph

East Fork

Dollarhide Summit

Deer Creek Road

Quigley Gulch Rd

Soldier Mt Ski Area Historic Site

Croy Creek Road

HAILEY

Muldoon Canyon Road

BELLEVUE

Fish Creek Reservoir

Big Wood River

Gannett

Little Wood Reservoir

20

Hill City

FAIRFIELD

Carey

To Boise

Picabo

Magic Reservoir

Silver Creek

Twin Lakes Reservoir

75

Richfield Canal

Little Wood River

To Twin Falls

How to Use This Guide

To use this book effectively, please note the following categorical descriptions.

Difficulty Ratings:

Easy: A typical beginner, fun, cruiser ride for most any ability.
Moderate: A bit harder than "easier" with most hills climbable, but not too technical.
Difficult: Fairly technical ride with tough climbs and descents. You will feel worked afterwards.
Abusive: The word speaks for itself, no matter the length of the ride. It is going to be hard, very technical, and you'll probably be in need of bandages.
Gonzo: In an effort to define a new category, this one is beyond abusive. This means, bring gear for a bivy, extra food, matches, water, and clothing.

Technical Ratings:

We rate our rides based on the technical aspect of it as well. This rating is numbered from 1 to 5. 1 is quite easy technically, while a rating of 5 means it is very technical, so be mentally and physically prepared.

Ride Details:

Distance: We would hope this is self-explanatory. However, all rides have cyclometer (mileage) readings. We also list as many features as possible so the people riding without a cyclometer won't get lost. In many cases, a GPS was also used to be sure ride stats are very accurate.
Difficulty rating: Just how aerobically and physically difficult the ride is.
Technical rating: Just how technical and challenging the ride is.
The ride: Defines the ride as an out-and-back, loop, or one-way.
Starting elevation: The elevation of the ride's starting point.
High point elevation: The highest point of the ride.
Total elevation gain: This is simply the difference between the high point and the low point.
Elevation gain/loss: This is the total gain and/or loss for the ride.
Surface: Explains the riding surface.
Season: Tells you what time of year the ride is in its best shape.
Fun factor: Key words to describe the highlights of the ride.
Summary: Brief description of the ride to get you psyched up!
Getting there: Tells you how to get to the trail.

Elevation Profiles

This book uses elevation profiles to provide an idea of the length and elevation of hills you will encounter along each ride. In each of the profiles the vertical axes of the graphs show the total distance climbed in feet. In contrast the horizontal axes show the distance traveled in miles. It is important to understand that the vertical (feet) and horizontal (miles) scales can differ between rides. Read the profile carefully, making sure you read both the height and distance shown. This will help you interpret what you see in each profile. Some elevation profiles may show gradual hills to be steep and steep hills to be gradual. Elevation profiles are not provided for rides with little or no elevation gain.

Route Maps

This is your primary guide to each ride. It shows all the access roads and trails, points of interest, water, towns, landmarks, and geographical features. It also distinguishes trails from roads and paved roads from unpaved roads. The selected route is highlighted, and directional arrows point the way.

Introduction

Idaho History and Wilderness

This part of central Idaho has a very rich history in mining. Around the lower part of the Wood River Valley (Ketchum, Hailey, Bellevue), you can see mining scars, tailings, and trails on the sides of some incredibly steep terrain. This is our mining past. Several rides in this guidebook lead to mining ghost towns such as Sawtooth City, Vienna, Custer, etc. In fact, back in the 1800s some of the populations of these mining communities were bigger than Ketchum is today.

Jacob's City was the first township in the Wood River Valley, settled in the fall of 1879 and was located between present-day Bellevue and Hailey. The next town settled was Ketchum, then Bullion (west of Hailey) and finally Bellevue in mid-1880. It wasn't until late 1880 that Hailey became a town, with all of the Wood River Valley towns centered around mining and the social scene that comes with prospering miners.

In the Stanley area, prospectors and hermits were a big part of the scene. They made their living by trying to strike it rich with their mining claims or just living in the wilderness year-round on the Middle Fork of the Salmon River. These hearty people led a rugged lifestyle, usually seeing other humans only once or twice a year.

Idaho is known as "The Wilderness State," although specific user groups have been trying to rename it "The Whitewater State." We have somewhere around twelve to thirteen million acres of wild lands around the state, ranging from national forest to Bureau of Land Management (BLM) to wilderness areas to simple roadless areas. Idaho actually has more wild land areas than any of the other lower forty-eight states.

The Sawtooth Mountains, in the heart of the Sawtooth National Wilderness Area by Stanley, are a huge attraction in the summertime, benefiting backpackers, rock and alpine climbers, and casual day hikers. However, these beautiful spires are not just for summer pleasure. They also offer great backcountry skiing in the winter and early springtime. But do take note: No mountain bikes or motorized vehicles are allowed in the Sawtooth Wilderness Area. So please respect the boundary signs and laws or Ranger Rick will be happy to do it for you. For more information on our local/state history, visit one of the bookstores in town. They all have a great selection and it's well worth your time getting to know the area you're playing in!

Weather and Lightning

In the springtime, the mountains can offer some of the most incredibly gorgeous scenery with wildflowers blooming and mountain streams flowing at full force. But don't be fooled by Mother Nature. June, July, and August in central Idaho have a history of afternoon thunderstorms that gather rapidly on the western horizon. Those small dark clouds in the distance can be upon you in no time, dumping rain, hail, and even snow. So be prepared for anything. Always bring a rain jacket, extra food, and water.

Lightning is another springtime worry in the mountains. "Oh, what are the chances?" you ask. Actually, the chance of getting struck by lightning is very remote, but possible. Take all the necessary precautions when you begin to hear thunder and see lightning. Lightning is usually at the leading edge of a storm where it is most violent. If you are not sure that electricity is in the air, check some obvious signs.

Take your helmet off and if your hair is standing on end, then yes, there is electricity in the area. You can also check the hair on your arms and smell ozone in the air. Obvious question here, what does ozone smell like? Much different than the clear mountain air you've been breathing, almost like a wet dog (we're not kidding). If you get caught in an electric storm, do the following: Make yourself small to minimize contact points with the ground (squat), get off any ridges, and get away from lone trees, lake shores, and rock outcroppings. If someone is struck by lightning (hopefully you know first aid), rush to get help. Due to the fact that we could get sued for telling you how to treat an injury, we can't say anything here.

Useful Web sites

Idaho Satellite Views: http://sat.wrh.noaa.gov/satellite/1km/Boise/VIS1BOI.GIF

Sawtooth National Forest Avalanche Center: http://www.avalanche.org/~svavctr

Stanley Web Camera: http://www.ruralnetwork.net/~dpinney

Sun Valley Ski Area Web Cameras: http://www.sunvalley.com/mountain/mountain_cams.cfm

Weather Forecast: www.crh.noaa.gov

Remember: DON'T GO OUT UNPREPARED FOR ANY EMERGENCY. You may be close to a town, but you are still miles away in a wild area and help can be just that much further away . . . "Be smart," as my dad would say.

Bugs and Animals

All of the rides in this guidebook are in the mountains where mosquitos, bees, and other flying (stinging) insects live. Most repellents work great at knocking them off their wings. In the later part of summer, look out for hornets and bees who tend to migrate toward open carbonated sugar drinks and beer. We also have a large population of big game animals. The elk, moose, deer, bears, wolves, foxes, coyotes, and all the other furry little creatures were here first. Remember that we are the ones playing in their homes and space. Please respect them and their privacy. Anyone caught harassing the animals will be stripped, tarred, and feathered and paraded up and down main street USA.

Tools/Clothing/Etc.

Hopefully, most of you are past getting dressed by your mothers each morning. Here is a small list of what to take just in case of some "interesting" weather.

Clothing: Rain or wind jacket, tights, gloves, cap, helmet, durable footwear, and an extra fleece layer. Remember, you're in the mountains here.

Tools: Extra tubes, pump, patches, chain tool, tire levers, allen wrenches, spoke wrench, screw driver (both kinds), and a small crescent wrench.

Miscellaneous Items: More food and water than you think you need, first aid kit, emergency blanket, and a camera (don't forget the film).

Helmet: ALWAYS, ALWAYS, ALWAYS!!!!!!!!!!!!!!!

Camping

Camping in the Sun Valley and Stanley area is relatively easy. There are pay campgrounds and there are "primitive" nonpay campgrounds. Most dirt roads off Highway 75 lead to some sort of primitive camping, while all of the pay campgrounds are labeled with official USFS signs. Most fees range anywhere from $7.00 to $10.00 per day. All campgrounds limit your stay, so plan on leaving . . . eventually. If you're looking for a primitive campsite, take any dirt road north of Ketchum and you should be fine unless signs indicate otherwise. Please respect others and all private property.

Showers/Food/Hot Springs

So you stink and are hungry? No worries, we've got the places for you to chill out. Food, of course, is readily available in all the surrounding towns, as are motels, phones, etc. This is only as primitive as a place as you want it to be. Showers are available at a small cost in a couple of areas: Redfish Lake, Easley Hot Springs, Sun Valley Athletic Club ($15 . . . ouch!). Hot springs are dotted along the Salmon River north, west, and east of Stanley, as well as up Warm Springs Road west of Ketchum. In Stanley, showers are available at Redfish Lake and Papa Brunee's in Stanley. A special note on the hot springs: don't pee, poop, litter, or detour the flow of or in any of the hot springs. Mother Nature put them here for us to enjoy, so please don't spoil it for the rest of the world.

Other Activities

Welcome to resort town life, where there are always activites happening to keep you busy when you're off the saddle or when it rains. There are four movie theaters between Ketchum and Hailey, bars everywhere, plenty of restaurants, horseback riding, world-famous whitewater kayaking, paragliding, rafting, and trails that offer great hiking to high alpine lakes. Don't forget your fishing gear. Fly-fishing is one of this area's main attractions. How about a round of golf on one of our world-class golf courses? Remember this is a destination resort designed to keep you and your money happy.

Mountain Biking Ethics

The Author's Version: Do unto others as you would want them to do unto you and your bike. In other words, don't be a jerk on the trails. Yield to everyone, uphill traffic, horses, hikers, and other cyclists. Treat our trails the way you eat in your mother's living room. Help others in need of tools, water, etc. This isn't the World Cup or Olympics; this is a peaceful place, so chill out, put your adrenaline aside, and relax.

The International Mountain Biking Association (IMBA) Version: Ride on open trails only. Practice zero-impact. Control your bicycle. Always yield the trail. Never spook animals. Plan ahead.

DO NOT SKID: This deteriorates and erodes the trails, making them useless. Push up or lower your bike down instead. Skidding around switchbacks is not the proper technique. Push your limits and when you reach the high end, push your bike.

DESCEND UNDER CONTROL: This will help you to avoid skidding, trail erosion, hitting another trail user, and an expensive trip to the emergency room (remember 911).

STAY OFF WET TRAILS: This does not only just pertain to "closed" trails in early season, since riding after a rain storm or snow melt can completely ruin a trail.

YIELD TO EVERYONE: Like it states above, this is a peaceful place we live in, so please be courteous to everyone or thing you encounter on the trails. Horses have very poor eyesight and are easily spooked. We have very poor eyesight and are easily spooked. Please be careful.

Please Sign in at All Trailheads

Please, please, please sign in at ALL trailheads throughout the Wood River, Sawtooth, and Copper Basin Valleys. The USFS can close ANY trail to mountain biking if they feel it is not being used for that sport very much. Therefore, we need you to help make mountain bikers "historical users" on all of these trails. The more the USFS sees mountain bikes being used, the less likely they are to close a trail. Please tell every mountain biker you see on the trails to sign in at the trailhead. Together, we can make a difference. That sounds familiar, must have heard it somewhere, sometime.

Want to Help with Our Trails?

Have you ever wanted to contribute either physically or financially to our extensive trail systems throughout the Wood River and Sawtooth Valleys? Well, now is your chance. Our local trail advocacy group, Big Wood Backcountry Trails, is constantly on the lookout for volunteers for trail clean-ups, reroutes, etc., etc. Send an e-mail to goodtrails@yahoo.com for more information.

Best Easy Rides

Adams Gulch Area - page 67
Corral Creek - page 55
Fox Creek - page 72
Galena Lodge Area - page 100

Best Date Rides

Adams Gulch Area - page 67
Galena Lodge Area - page 100

Best Gonzo/Hard Rides

Bowery Loop - page 107
Fox Peak - page 80
Little Boulder to Big Boulder Loop - page 130
Wyoming Creek - page 124

Best Night Rides

Adams Gulch Area - page 67
Bald Mountain Trails - page 63
Chocolate Gulch - page 74
Fisher Creek - page 112
Fox Creek - page 72

Our Favorite Sun Valley Rides

Bowery Loop - page 107
Elk Mountain - page 118
Lake Creek (Copper Basin) - page 87
Little Boulder to Big Boulder Loop - page 130
Park Creek - page 85
Potato Mountain Loop (Little Basin Creek) - page 126
Redfish Lake Loop - page 114
Winnemucca Creek-Beaver Creek Loop - page 122

Multiday and Adventurous Rides

1. Norton Creek to Big Smoky: Starting in the Baker Creek drainage north of Ketchum, ride up and over Norton Creek into the Big Smoky drainage, eventually coming out at the Skillern Hot Springs and Big Smoky Campground, close to Featherville in the South Fork of Boise River drainage.

2. North Fork of Big Lost River to Bowery Hot Springs: Near the end of the North Fork of Big Lost River Road, head north to Hunter Creek Summit. From here you'll descend into East Pass Creek and then to Bowery Creek. From the East Fork of Salmon River Road, turn left and ride up to the hot springs.

3. Alturas Lake to Atlanta: From Alturas Lake on the southern end of the Sawtooth Mountains, ride up and over into the Ross Fork Basin toward Ross Fork Lakes. Turn northwest into Decker Creek drainage and follow this into Atlanta. (There are other variations to this adventure; check with the USFS for trail improvements, etc.)

4. Little Casino to Big Casino Loop: This trail will be getting some improvements in the coming years, so put it on your to-do list for the near future. Add in Boundary Creek for some climbing anaerobic fun!

5. Boundary to Williams Creek: From Highway 75 near the Sawtooth Fish Hatchery, follow Boundary Creek up and over the ridgeline heading east and eventually coming out near The Meadows in Warm Springs Creek. You can either ride out north to the Salmon River or south to finish up on Fisher Creek.

6. Ants Basin Loop: Park at the white cliffs up Fourth of July Creek Road and ride up and over the summit into Ants Basin. Take the link back to Fisher Creek and ride down Fisher Creek Road to the spur trail that will link you back to your car at the white cliffs. Amazing ride!

7. Basin Butte Area: You can ride all over the Basin Butte area just north and west of Stanley. There are singletrack linkages everywhere. Try Valley Creek to Prospect Creek to East Fork of Valley Creek, or throw in a little bit of Sunday Creek to the Potato Mountain Loop. The world is your oyster up here!

8. Lick Creek: Just over Dollarhide Summit out Warm Springs Creek you'll find a one-way trail called Lick Creek. The USFS will be doing improvements on this trail in the near future.

9. Middle Fork to South Fork of Warm Springs: This has been a heinous linkage in the past, but now the USFS is creating huge trail improvements (summer 2001). The resulting ride will be a loop topping out on the ridge looking down into the Willow Creek drainage before looping around to Poison Flat and back to the start.

10. Johnstone Creek to Pioneer Cabin Loop: This is not a very popular trail and not particularly well-suited for mountain bikes. Keep this in mind when you're pushing and walking your bike. Start out Hyndman Creek up East Fork Canyon and ride up Johnstone Creek to Pioneer Cabin. From there, ride/walk down the east side of the cabin into the North Fork of Hyndman Creek and back to your car. Save this for when you've done everything else.

11. Hailey to Copper Basin Loop: From Hailey, ride out Quigley Canyon, up and over into the Little Wood River drainage. Turn up Porcupine Creek and into the headwaters of the Little Wood River. Drop down to the Copper Creek Trail and into Copper Basin. How you get back is up to you.

12. Hindman Lake: From Basin Creek Campground on the Salmon River, ride up the creek to Hindman Lake. From there, you can either ride back down the same way, or take the trail to Basin Butte, eventually coming down Nip & Tuck Trail outside Stanley. This would be a very long one-day ride. Always have a back-up plan.

13. Couch Summit to Big Smoky: From the top of Couch Summit by the Soldier Mountains, follow the jeep road across the ridges before dropping down into Miller Creek just outside of the Big Smoky Campground.

14. The Warm Springs Trail: From Bull Trout Lake outside Stanley on Highway 20, follow Dead Man Creek (Warm Springs Trail) all the way down to Bonneville Hot Springs. Don't be fooled into thinking this is an easy downhill ride, or you'll really get worked!

Map Legend

Symbols

Airport	✈	Peak	▲
Animal Shelter	🐾	Picnic Area	⛉
Bridge	≍	Point of Interest	▪
Campground/ Campsite	⚑	Ranger Station/ Park Office	👪
Cemetery	†	Trailend	●
Falls/Rapids	∥	Trailhead	🚴
Gate	•—•	Shelter	⊏
Hot Springs	♨	Ski Area	⛷
Lodge	⌂	Springs	⌐
Mine	⚒	Store	⬆
Pass	)(	Visitor Center/ Information	❓
Parking	🅟		

Transportation

U. S. Highway	═⟨27⟩═
State Highway	═⟨75⟩═
Primary Road	▬▬▬
Forest Road	═[138]═
Improved Road	═══
Unimproved Road	= = = = =
Trail	··········

Hydrology

Lake/Reservoir	
River/Creek	

Riding in the South Valley Area

The first singletrack trails to open each year are those in the South Valley area. That usually means late March in a typical year, but mostly open by the middle of April. Your best bet for early season riding is the south-facing rides and dirt roads. As the season gets warmer, the riding gets a bit dusty down there and it can get increasingly hot as the days move on. Prepare for warmth and weather.

There are more and more trails being created in this area each season, so if you encounter a trail not mentioned on the ride list or overview map, chances are that it's a new one. Turn onto it and give it a roll; you never know where you'll end up, but chances are that you'll have an incredible time. In the more southern part of the valley, you'll find loads of jeep roads, especially out in the desert. These are phenomenal early-season rides for getting the blood pumping back into your burned-out ski legs. Be careful out there by June, as the rattlers like to bask in and around the lava rocks!

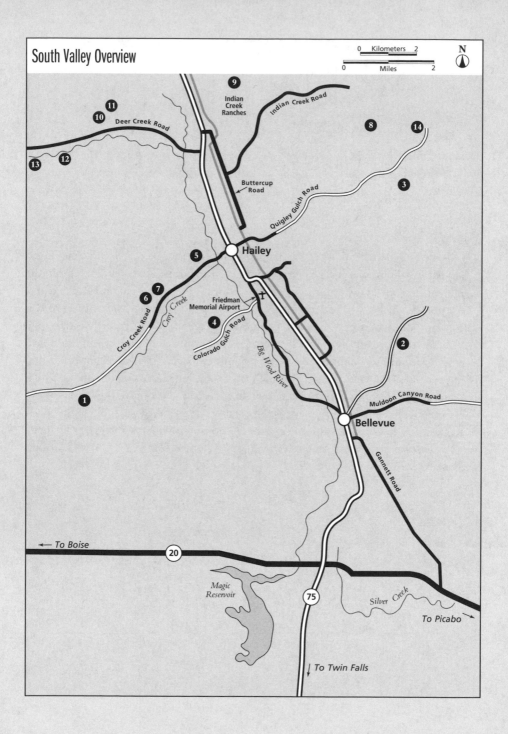

South Valley Overview

Kilometers
0 — 2

Miles
0 — 2

N

⑨ Indian Creek Ranches

Indian Creek Road

⑪
⑩ Deer Creek Road

⑧ ⑭

⑬ ⑫

Buttercup Road

③

Quigley Gulch Road

⑤ **Hailey**

⑦
⑥ Croy Creek

Croy Creek Road

Friedman Memorial Airport
④ Colorado Gulch Road

Big Wood River

②

①

Muldoon Canyon Road

Bellevue

Gannett Road

To Boise ←

20

Magic Reservoir

75

Silver Creek

To Picabo →

↓ To Twin Falls

1 Hatty Gulch

This is the locals' standard, early-season ride to get their legs and butt into shape. It's a fast cruise with a bit of climbing, mostly on jeep roads.

Distance: 26.2 miles
Difficulty rating: Moderate
Technical rating: 2
The ride: Loop
Starting elevation: 5,300 feet
High point elevation: 6,000 feet

Total elevation gain: 1,110 feet
Surface: Dirt jeep road, pavement, singletrack
Season: Late April through late November
Fun factor: Serene sagebrush desert setting with cow pies, snakes, and water

Getting there: From Main Street in Hailey, turn left (west) onto Bullion Street at the street light and go 1.5 blocks to Hop Porter Park. This is where the ride begins. Drive to the junction with Rock Creek Road and begin the ride there if you are looking for a shorter ride.

Miles and Directions

0.0 Begin by riding out Croy Creek Road on the pavement, passing through housing areas and the BMX track. Watch for Rotorun Ski Area on the right.

3.7 The pavement ends and the dirt road begins. Stay straight on this road.

4.1 Pass by Rock Creek Road on the left. Stay straight; this is where you complete the loop.

9.1 Just before starting to climb up Richardson Summit, turn left and follow this road down, passing by a DANGER, OPEN MINES sign.

9.3 Turn right on the switchback and follow the road down into the main gulch following the stream bed. You will follow this main Hatty Gulch all the way to the junction with Rock Creek Road. There may be new fencing, bad ruts, and cows in your way, but stick to the road that follows the stream flow and you'll be fine.

18.5 The junction with Rock Creek Road. Turn left and begin some gradual climbing up toward Rocky Butte. Stay on this main road all the way up and over.

22.1 The junction with Croy Creek Road. Your loop is complete. Follow Croy Creek Road back to Hailey.

26.2 Back at Hop Porter Park in Hailey and a job well done.

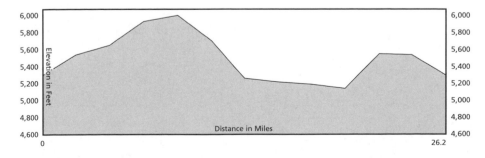

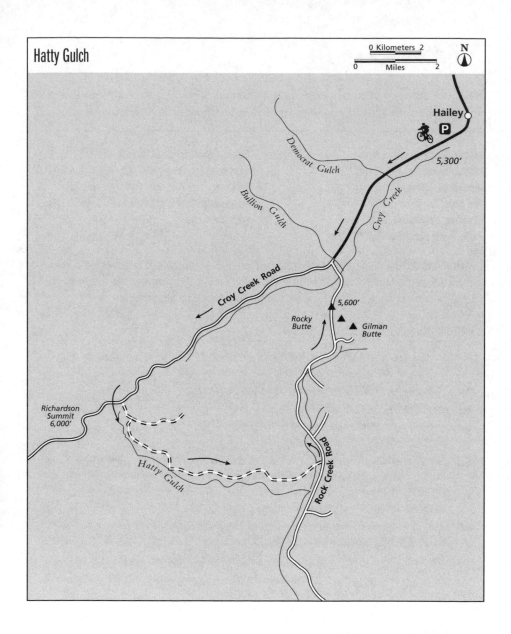

Hatty Gulch

Hailey

5,300'

Democrat Gulch

Bullion Gulch

Croy Creek

Croy Creek Road

5,600'

Rocky
Butte

Gilman
Butte

Richardson
Summit
6,000'

Hatty Gulch

Rock Creek Road

0 Kilometers 2

0 Miles 2

N

2 Slaughterhouse Creek

This is a casual ride through a southern canyon with alpine meadows, groves of aspens, and five quick stream crossings (just to add a bit of excitement).

Distance: 13 miles
Difficulty rating: Easy
Technical rating: 2 (creeks)
The ride: Out-and-back
Starting elevation: 5,230 feet
High point elevation: 6,200 feet

Total elevation gain: 970 feet
Surface: Dirt jeep road
Season: April through November
Fun factor: Beautiful canyon with alpine meadows

Getting there: From Hailey, drive south on Highway 75 to Bellevue and turn left (east) on Cedar Street, which is the street next to the old white building with a steeple that looks like an old church but is really the old Bellevue City Hall. Stay straight on this road, crossing the bike path and the elementary school on the left. Drive to the top of the hill and park anywhere out of the way of the road and driveways. The ride begins here.

Miles and Directions

0.0 Begin by riding up the north side of the canyon.

0.2 Spur road on the right, stay straight.

1.4 Steep spur road takes off on the left that eventually hooks up with the spur road that takes off on the left at mile 1.5. Stay on the main road here.

2.7 A few springs muddy up the road a bit here (not bad). After some big shade trees, motor up a steep climb. From here the road crosses the creek five times over the next 2 miles.

4.8 You're at the last of the stream crossings.

5.0 Spur road up the canyon on the right; stay on the main road.

5.7 After the canyon narrows, it opens again fairly soon.

6.5 Fork in the road and the top of the ride for those of you joining us for the out-and-back portion of the movie. Those of you who want to call it good, turn around and ride the 6.5

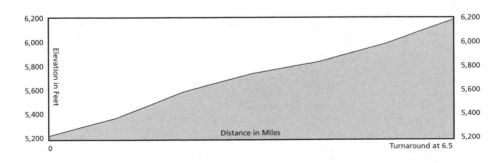

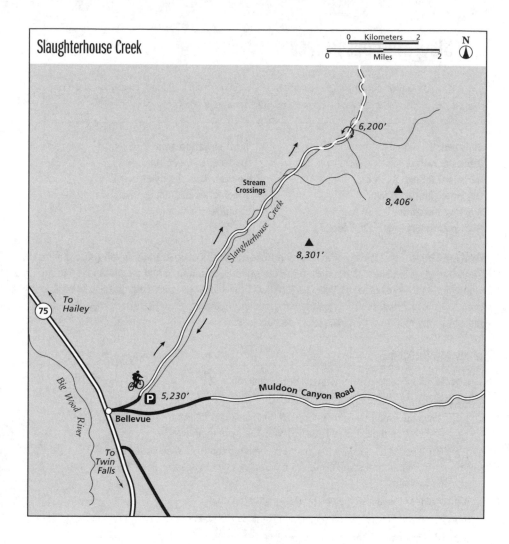

Slaughterhouse Creek

Stream
Crossings

6,200'

8,406'

8,301'

Slaughterhouse Creek

To
Hailey

75

Big Wood River

Muldoon Canyon Road

5,230'

Bellevue

To
Twin
Falls

miles back to the trailhead . . . thanks for playing. The left fork continues up the drainage (very rutted) to the saddle with Quigley Creek and down into Hailey. The right fork meanders up to where it is too steep to ride. The ugly trail quickly turns to loose rocks and scree and ends at a small saddle with questionable views as to whether or not it's worth it. See Quigley Creek to Slaughterhouse Creek for more information.

13.0 Back at your car in Bellevue.

3 Quigley Creek to Slaughterhouse Creek

This is a great nontechnical ride with moderate elevation gain near the top end. If this were aerobics, it would be classified as "low-impact."

Distance: 19.2 miles
Difficulty rating: Moderate/Difficult
Technical rating: 2+ (rutted downhill)
The ride: Loop
Starting elevation: 5,350 feet
High point elevation: 6,950 feet

Total elevation gain: 1,600 feet
Surface: Dirt jeep road
Season: April through November
Fun factor: Easy rolling ride through a southern canyon setting with good climbing

Getting there: From the stoplight at Bullion Street and Highway 75 in downtown Hailey, drive 1 block south to Croy Street and turn left. After 0.5 mile, follow the road around a natural right turn and take an immediate left onto Quigley Road, which is directly in front of the DEERFIELD sign. Continue forward to where the pavement turns to dirt and park here. (**Note:** You can ride on singletrack for quite a ways up Quigley right from the parking area.) The singletrack parallels the road just past the parking area on the left and ends at the cattle guard by the pond, then starts up again to the right, just after the fence by the pond and goes to the corrals. Don't miss out on this fun part of the canyon!

Miles and Directions

0.0 Begin riding up Quigley Gulch Road, heading east alongside a large field and across the cattle guard.

2.2 Small spur road on the right; continue straight on Quigley Gulch Road.

2.5 The spur road rejoins the main road.

4.2 Pass a corral then a spur road just a bit further on the left side.

5.8 Spur road on the left leads to/from Indian Creek. Continue up the main road curving to the south up and through some clear cuts. Always stay on the main road through this area.

7.8 At the fork in the road before a small creek (possibly dry in mid to late summer), turn right on the spur road, traversing back across the hillside. If you were to turn left or stay on the main road here, you would be on the Quigley Creek to Cove Creek ride.

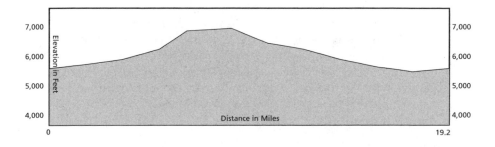

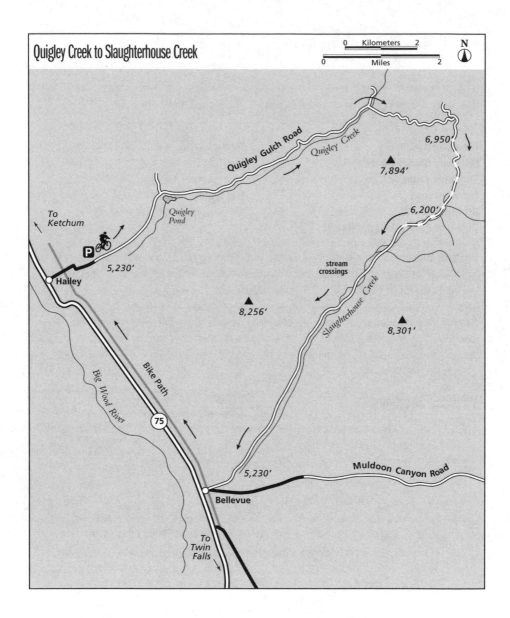

8.3 You've reached the saddle overlooking Slaughterhouse Creek. Continue.

9.5 After crossing the small creek, stay to the right heading down the canyon toward Bellevue. For the next 6.5 miles, you'll have many stream crossings and a few mud-bogs, otherwise it's a straight shot down the canyon into Bellevue.

16.0 The end of the dirt road and the town of Bellevue. Continue down Cedar Street until you get to the Wood River Bike Trail. Turn right. Ride approximately 3.2 miles into Hailey and turn right on Croy Street and retrace your steps to your car at the mouth of Quigley Creek.

19.2 End of the loop, and back at your car.

4 Colorado Gulch

If you have a need for a very quick workout to kill some of that daily stress, jump on this ride and pump 'til you puke!

Distance: 8.2 miles
Difficulty rating: Moderate/Difficult
Technical rating: 2+ (lungs)
The ride: Loop
Starting elevation: 5,300 feet
High point elevation: 6,250 feet

Total elevation gain: 950 feet
Surface: Dirt jeep road and pavement
Season: Mid-April through November
Fun factor: A quick pump, a quick downhill, and you're back on the couch

Getting there: From the stoplight at Bullion Street and Highway 75 in downtown Hailey, park 1 block behind Blockbuster Video at Hop Porter Park. The ride begins here.

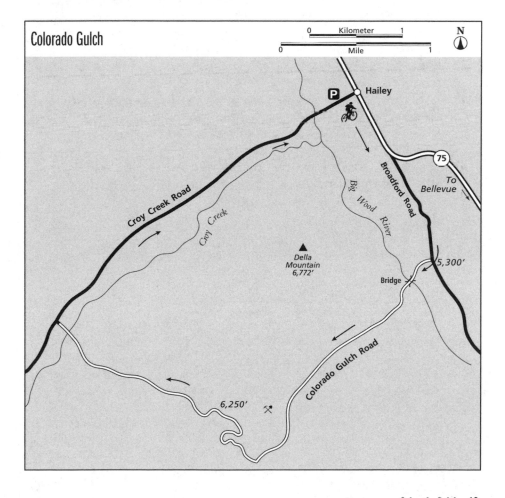

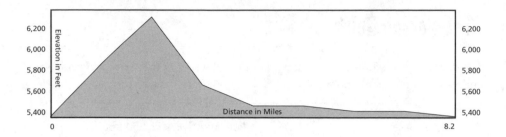

Miles and Directions

0.0 Begin by riding back up to Main Street in Hailey (Highway 75) and head south toward the airport. Turn right on Cedar Street, just before the post office, then take a quick left onto Broadford Road. Go 0.8 miles and turn right on a dirt road. (Don't take the right just before the old, abandoned wood house. Instead take the second, more beaten dirt road after the old wood house). Go down the road, veering left and crossing the bridge over the Big Wood River and begin climbing through aspens next to the creek.

2.8 After passing several spur roads on either side of the road, pass a mine and old buildings on the left.

3.8 With some steady climbs behind you, the trail levels out for a spell before climbing again, and oh baby, does it climb!

4.1 Top of the ride. Congrats! Catch your breath and get ready for a speedy ride downhill. Check your brakes first.

5.5 Junction with Croy Creek Road. Turn right (east) back toward Hailey, staying on Croy Creek Road.

8.2 Just after crossing the Big Wood River, you'll see Hop Porter Park on the left and your car. This is the end of the ride.

5 Carbonate Mountain Trail

A fairly new trail in Hailey gets action early in the season, during lunch hours and post-work for those dying to get a quick workout in legs and lungs!

Distance: 6.2 miles
Difficulty rating: Moderate/Difficult
Technical rating: 2+ (skinny trail and lungs)
The ride: Out-and-back or loop option
Starting elevation: 5,300 feet
High point elevation: 6,720 feet

Total elevation gain: 1,420 feet
Surface: Singletrack, dirt jeep road, and pavement
Season: Late April through Early November
Fun factor: Blow your lungs and legs out on a local "test" piece with killer views

Getting there: From the stoplight at Bullion Street and Highway 75 in downtown Hailey, park 1 block behind Blockbuster Video at Hop Porter Park. The ride begins here.

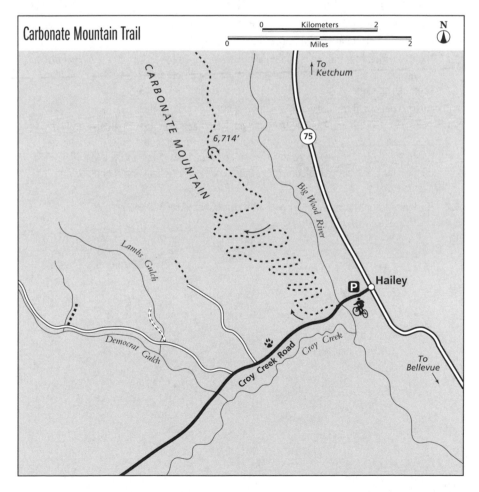

Carbonate Mountain Trail

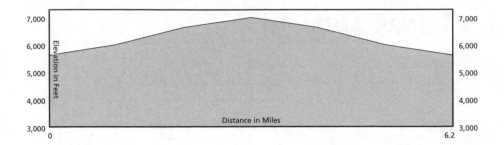

Miles and Directions

0.0 From the stoplight in Hailey, head west on Bullion Street, quickly crossing over the Big Wood River.

0.1 You'll most likely see cars parked on the right side of the road next to the river and in front of a wooden fence. Lift your bike over the fence and start up the trail leading to the east and up.

0.2 Stay on the singletrack that does NOT head straight up the ridge.

0.3 After a small climb, the trail now starts to switchback to the top.

2.1 The trail heads over the small saddle and crosses a jeep road. Stay on the singletrack as it switchbacks on the east side of the slope for a bit before heading back over to the south-facing slopes.

2.8 The trail heads up the ridge, slightly steeper, but definitely doable.

3.1 The top of the ride and Carbonate Mountain. From here you can turn around and go back down the way you came up. Or you could continue along the ridge trail heading north. Should you choose to go this way, go up to the powerlines and you just might find a little surprise: A singletrack downhill at the end. Please be conscious of our bovine friends along the way.

6.2 Back down from Carbonate and back at your car, hopefully well-winded.

6 Democrat Gulch

So, you need a change of pace from that boring singletrack riding? This is it. Casual or difficult, you make the choice; either one is well worth it.

Distance: 12.4 miles
Difficulty rating: Moderate/Difficult to top, or Easy to first turn-around.
Technical rating: 2+ (rocks and lungs)
The ride: Out-and-back
Starting elevation: 5,300 feet
High point elevation: 6,750 feet

Total elevation gain: 750 feet or 1,450 feet (750 feet to the first turn-around)
Surface: Pavement to dirt jeep road
Season: Early April through late October
Fun factor: Small but beautiful creek, Pioneer Mountain views, wildflowers

Getting there: From the stoplight at Bullion Street and Highway 75 in downtown Hailey, park 1 block behind Blockbuster Video at Hop Porter Park. The ride begins here.

Miles and Directions

0.0 From the stoplight in Hailey, head west on Bullion Street, quickly crossing over the Big Wood River.

1.2 You are now in Croy Creek Canyon and passing by the Wood River Animal Shelter.

1.7 Turn right onto Democrat Gulch Road and wind up the side of a small hill. There may or may not be other cars parked at this make-shift trailhead.

2.0 A gravel road enters in from the left. Stay on main road heading north.

2.9 Spur road on the right goes up Lambs Gulch. Notice a small pond on the left. Remember, stay on the main road.

3.9 Spur road on the right; don't take it.

4.1 Beaver ponds on the left.

4.7 Enter into the rocky corridor; you'll know what we mean.

5.0 Cross over the creek on an exposed pipe.

5.2 Fork in the road after crossing over the creek. Take the right fork and begin a gradual climb to the top (the left road goes nowhere) you're at 6,050 feet. This can also be a turnaround point for the more casual version of this ride. Or continue on up.

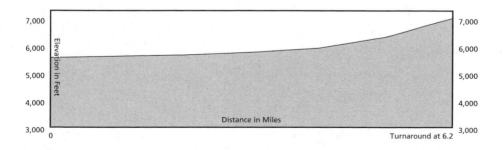

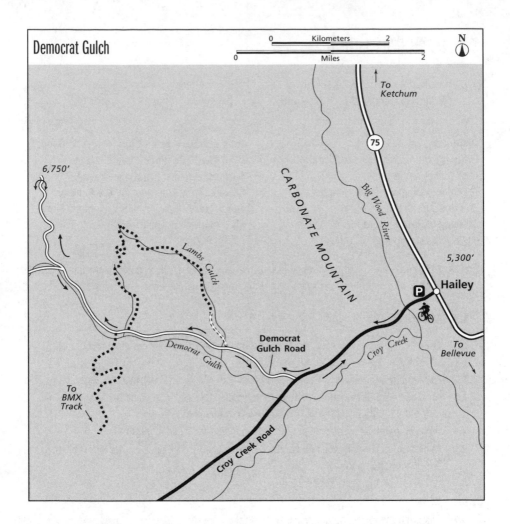

6.2 This is the top of the ride. You can check out the Pioneer Mountains to the east, or explore the other trails up here. Be careful descending back down the gulch and into Hailey. (**Note:** The trail heading down the north side of this saddle leads to private property in Deer Creek. Please do not go down.)

12.4 Back in Hailey and the end of the ride.

7 Lambs Gulch Loop

Close to Hailey singletrack that'll get your heart pounding, your legs burning, and a smile on your face.

Distance: 8.4 miles
Difficulty rating: Moderate
Technical rating: 2+
The ride: Loop
Starting elevation: 5,300 feet

High point elevation: 6,220 feet
Total elevation gain: 1,050 feet
Surface: Dirt jeep road, singletrack, pavement
Fun factor: Good for early season and late fall in a peaceful setting

Getting there: From the stoplight at Bullion Street and Highway 75 in downtown Hailey, drive west into the large canyon aptly named Croy Canyon. At 1.7 miles, park on the right side of the road next to the dirt road and fence. Please don't block the road. The ride begins here. (**Option:** You could also start this ride at Hop Porter Park in Hailey by the river.)

Miles and Directions

0.0 Begin by riding up the dirt road (quick hill) that you parked next to. Stay on this road for the next 1 mile.

1.0 Turn right just past the trees onto a jeep road that crosses the stream soon thereafter.

2.0 After crossing a cattle guard then another stream, stay left at the next junction.

2.5 In the small clearing a jeep road goes up and left and a jeep road goes up and right. Instead, take the singletrack that follows along the right side of the creek bed. After roughly 0.2 mile, take a sharp left turn into the aspens and begin a meandering climb up to the top.

2.9 At the saddle where the trails all join up, turn right (west) and head down on a faint jeep road that turns to singletrack shortly. On the grassy hill, make your way down the semi-nonexistent trail to the grove of trees. There, you will find a better singletrack trail leading left into the trees and down the canyon on the east side of the creek.

3.8 Junction with Democrat Gulch Road. Turn right here.

3.9 Whoa! Look for the singletrack dropping down to the left and crossing the creek, which is located where the willows are closest to the road.

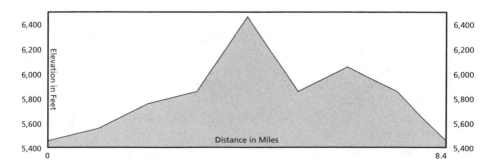

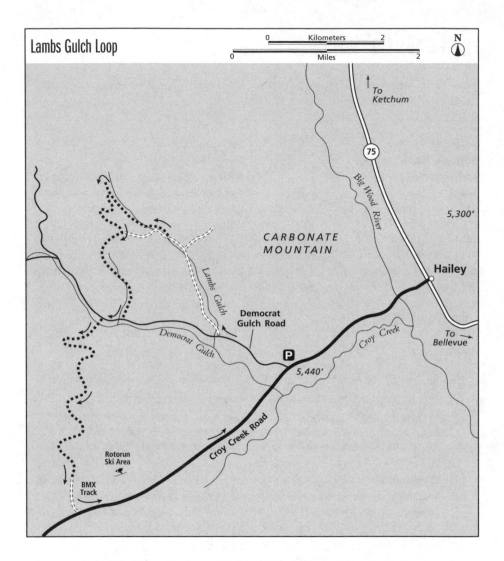

4.3 The top of the first saddle. The trail forks shortly afterwards. Both trails lead to the same place a hundred yards later, but be careful of loose rocks.

4.9 Cross over the dry stream bed and follow the faint trail leading left and up.

5.1 Top of the second saddle. Careful for the sharp turn on the descent.

5.6 In the clearing with houses down to the left, stay straight and continue traversing up on the doubletrack jeep road.

5.8 Top of the last saddle overlooking the BMX track area. There are many trails all over the place as you descend. Stay on the most popular path, which veers left and east across the back of the BMX track.

6.5 Junction with Croy Creek Road. Turn left and follow this road back to your car at the start of Democrat Gulch Road.

8.4 Yep, you're here, the end of the ride. Nice job!

8 Quigley Creek to Indian Creek

This can be as intense as you make it. Stop often on the climb and enjoy yourself, or abuse yourself and do it nonstop. Once the climb is over, this is an amazing downhill all the way back to Hailey.

Distance: 19.2 miles
Difficulty rating: Moderate/Difficult
Technical rating: 2+ (loose scree coming down Indian Creek)
The ride: Loop
Starting elevation: 5,397 feet

High point elevation: 7,310 feet
Total elevation gain: 1,913 feet
Surface: Pavement and dirt jeep road
Season: Late April through October
Fun factor: Fun hill-climbs, killer views, and an awesome descent

Getting there: From the stoplight at Bullion Street and Highway 75 in downtown Hailey, drive 1 block south to Croy Street and turn left. After 0.5 mile, follow the road around a natural right turn and take an immediate left onto Quigley Gulch Road, which is directly in front of the DEER-FIELD sign. Continue forward to where the pavement turns to dirt and park here. (**Note:** You can ride on singletrack for quite a ways up Quigley right from the parking area. The singletrack parallels the road just past the parking area on the left and ends at the cattle guard by the pond, then starts up again to the right, just after the fence by the pond and goes to the corrals. Don't miss out on this fun part of the canyon!)

Miles and Directions

0.0 Begin riding up Quigley Gulch Road heading east alongside a large field and across the cattle guard.

1.75 Pass Quigley Pond on the right side of the road.

2.2 Small spur road on the right; continue straight on Quigley Gulch Road.

2.5 The spur road rejoins the main road.

4.2 Pass a corral then a spur road just a bit farther on the left side.

5.8 Turn left at the fork, which leads to Indian Creek.

6.0 Begin slowly climbing up the canyon. Pace yourself!

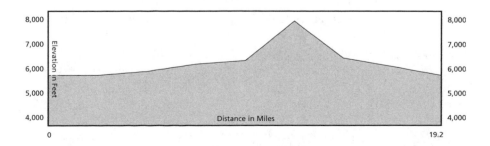

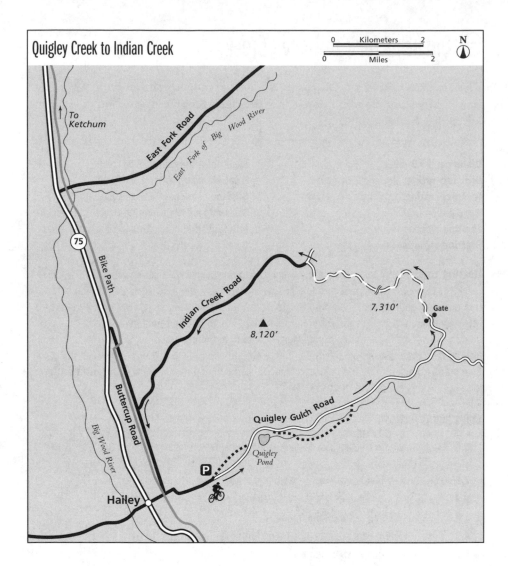

Quigley Creek to Indian Creek

8.5 Spur road to the left. Don't take it; it leads to private property.

8.8 The top of the climbing. Take in the views and breathe. Descend the main road all the way to pavement. Take note: There are side roads along the way.

13.0 Dirt ends and pavement begins. Follow the main road all the way down Indian Creek until the junction with Buttercup Road.

16.2 Buttercup Road. Cross over it and ride on the bike path heading south.

18.2 Bike path intersects Croy Street. Turn left on Croy Street and retrace your steps back to your car.

19.2 Your car. You're worked. You're happy?!

9 Ohio Gulch

If you're in the mood for a nice evening or morning pump, this is the ride for you. Beautiful views of the Ohio Gulch Transfer Station (county dump), and the Pioneer and Smoky Mountains.

Distance: 14.6 miles
Difficulty rating: Moderate/Difficult
Technical rating: 1
The ride: Out-and-back
Starting elevation: 5,620 feet
High point elevation: 7,870 feet

Total elevation gain: 2,250 feet
Surface: Dirt jeep road
Season: Late April through October
Fun factor: Great views, beautiful canyon setting, and a killer pump

Getting there: From Ketchum, drive south on Highway 75 for 6.8 miles and turn left on Ohio Gulch Road. Immediately park on the right side of the road in the gravel next to the bike path. This is where the ride begins. (**Note:** You can also drive up Ohio Gulch Road the 1.8 miles to where the gravel road begins and skip the pavement portion of the ride.)

Miles and Directions

0.0 Ride up Ohio Gulch Road heading toward the foothills.

1.0 The Gun Club appears on the left. Stay on the road toward the transfer station.

1.8 The transfer station turn-off is on the left. Keep straight and continue onto the gravel road, which begins weaving around and behind the transfer station. The right fork leads overland to the Indian Creek subdivision.

2.9 View point of the upper transfer station and beginning of a quick, rocky downhill. At the bottom of the downhill, continue on the main jeep road to the right.

3.2 Gain a small saddle and prepare for some climbing ahead.

3.8 Encounter a small steep hill—a tough climb.

4.1 Begin a scree-slope hill climb, one of a series to come.

4.3 Gain another small saddle and get ready to climb again.

5.0 The first of a few switchbacks starts here with moderate to easy climbing between them.

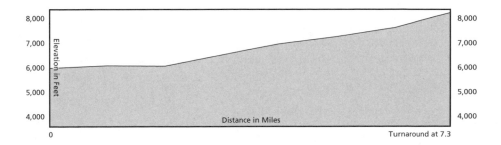

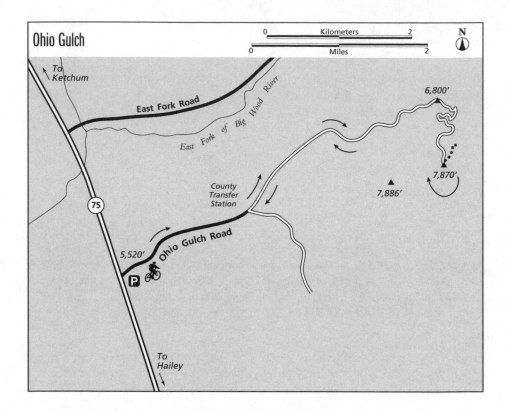

Ohio Gulch

To Ketchum

East Fork Road

East Fork of Big Wood River

County Transfer Station

75

Ohio Gulch Road

5,520'

P

6,800'

7,870'

7,886'

To Hailey

5.9 Come into a clearing with awesome views of the Smoky Mountains to the west. Continue up a series of switchbacks and moderate climbing with a steep hill climb to gain the summit saddle.

7.3 The top! Incredible views of the Pioneer Mountains and the canyons of Indian and Quigley Creeks. Take some pictures, suck in some air, enjoy the views and get ready for a fast downhill! There is a small singletrack leading off to the east, which goes around the small knob. It eventually leads down into the Indian Creek area and/or Cove Creek drainage.

14.6 End of the ride and (hopefully) back to your car.

10 North Fork of Deer Creek

The best part of this ride is getting the climbing done first and having a killer downhill for more than 6 miles. Killer views and tons of wildlife!

Distance: 11.3 miles
Difficulty rating: Difficult
Technical rating: 4 (all on the descent)
The ride: Loop
Starting elevation: 5,970 feet
High point elevation: 7,440 feet

Total elevation gain: 1,470 feet
Surface: Dirt jeep road and singletrack trail
Season: Early June through late October
Fun factor: Beautiful creeks, wildflowers, and high alpine meadows

Getting there: From Ketchum, drive south on Highway 75 for 10.9 miles and turn right at the forest service sign for DEER CREEK ROAD. Follow this road for just over 10 miles to the junction with

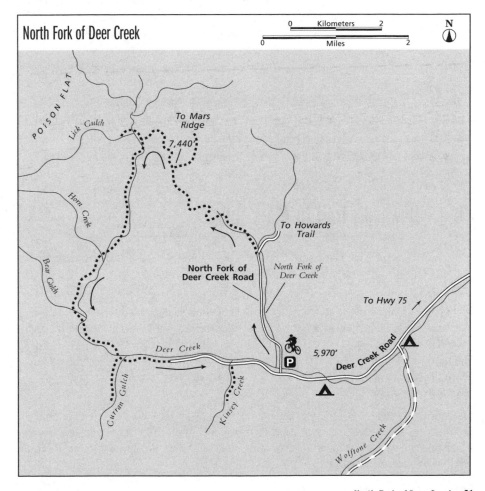

North Fork of Deer Creek

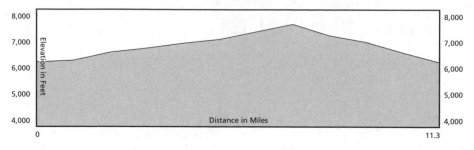

North Fork of Deer Creek and park on the left off the road at this junction. This is where the ride begins.

Miles and Directions

0.0 Begin by riding up the North Fork of Deer Creek Road.

1.6 Take the left fork at the trailhead leading up a singletrack trail.

4.0 The top of the ride at the trail junction. Continue on down the other side toward Poison Flat. The right fork leads to Mars Ridge.

4.4 A small pond is located in the trees here. Not good swimming, but good wildlife viewing possibilities.

4.9 Trail junction. Take the left fork leading down the Deer Creek drainage. The right fork goes toward Poison Flat.

9.0 Pass by Curran Gulch trailhead on the right. Stay on the main trail down.

10.1 Primitive hunting campsite and the start of the jeep road and the end of the singletrack.

10.7 Pass by the Kinsey Creek trailhead on the right. Stay on the jeep road down.

11.3 You just rode past your car. Hey, hey, turn around, that was the end of the ride.

11 Howard's Trail to Mars Ridge

This is an aerobic ride with some grinding and killer downhills. Bring extra food, water, a jacket, and a camera. You'll want and use them all!

Distance: 12.1 miles
Difficulty rating: Difficult/Abusive
Technical rating: 3+
The ride: Loop
Starting elevation: 6,360 feet
High point elevation: 8,525 feet

Total elevation gain: 2,165 feet
Surface: Dirt jeep road and singletrack trail
Season: June through late October
Fun factor: 360-degree views of the entire area, wildflowers, and a moonscape

Getting there: From Ketchum, drive south on Highway 75 for 10.9 miles and turn right at the forest service sign for DEER CREEK ROAD. Follow this road for just over 10 miles to the junction with North Fork of Deer Creek. Turn right and go another 1.6 miles. Park on the left near the trailhead sign. This is where the ride begins.

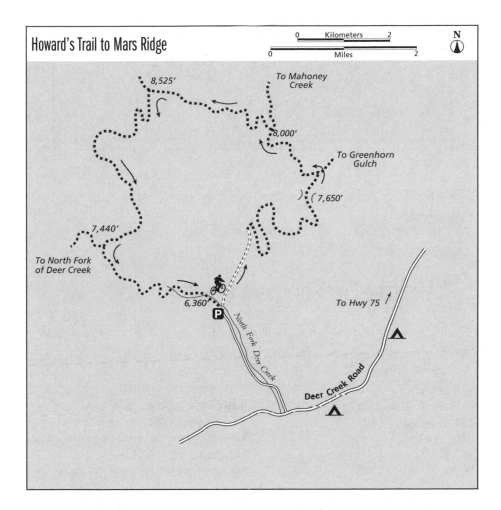

Miles and Directions

0.0 Begin by riding up the jeep road following the sign to Howard's Trail.

1.3 The jeep road ends at a small creek crossing. From here it's all singletrack up the switch-backs to the next junction. All rideable, never too steep.

3.9 The junction with Greenhorn Gulch. Turn left and continue climbing up.

5.0 Another junction at a saddle. Turn left and continue more climbing. It gets a bit steeper here and you may have to walk a little bit. Well worth it!

5.7 You are now on the famous Mars Ridge; enjoy the scenery and ride on.

7.3 Now that you're done riding along the ridge, turn left at the junction and start the descent into the North Fork of Deer Creek.

8.6 You now drop into the trees leaving the upper bowl and ridge behind.

9.8 Junction with North Fork of Deer Creek Trail. Turn left (south) and begin an incredibly fun switchback descent (that is, if you didn't think the past 2 miles have been a hoot!).

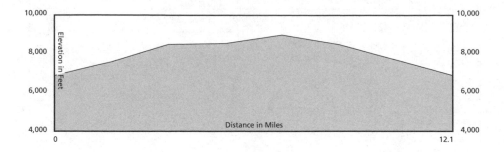

(**Note:** You could also turn right and complete the remainder of the North Fork of Deer Creek ride.)

12.1 The single track has ended right at your car. Wow, that was awesome!

12 Wolftone Creek to Kinsey Creek

This ride rivals any in the area for fun, challenge, and views. (**FYI:** Another option for this ride is to ride to the saddle next to Kelly Mountain and down into Croy Creek. The turn-off for that ride is at mile 5 listed below.)

Distance: 8.1 miles
Difficulty rating: Difficult
Technical rating: 3+
The ride: Loop
Starting elevation: 5,850

High point elevation: (see "Note")
Total elevation gain: (see "Note")
Surface: Dirt jeep road and singletrack trail
Season: June through October
Fun factor: Views, views, and more views

(**Note:** This ride may be combined with Kinsey Creek to to Curran Gluch. The combined High Point elevations and total elevation gain are listed on page 36.)

Getting there: From Ketchum, drive south on Highway 75 for approximately 9 miles and turn right at the forest service sign for DEER CREEK ROAD. Follow this road for just over 8 miles and park on the left by the sign for WOLFTONE CREEK.

Miles and Directions

0.0 Begin the ride by heading up Wolftone Creek Road.

1.1 After gaining a small hill on mining tailings, follow the road as it turns west and heads up the canyon.

2.7 Spur road and a cabin on the right leads nowhere too exciting. Continue to ride forward.

3.9 End of the road and beginning of singletrack trail. Continue riding up the valley. DO NOT take the trail that crosses the creek and switches back to the left. Stay right and go straight up the drainage.

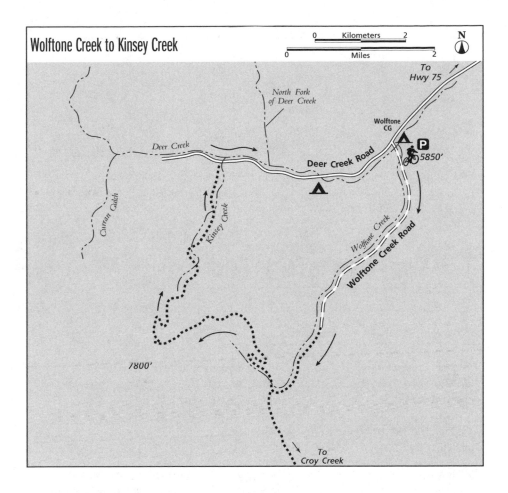

Wolftone Creek to Kinsey Creek

4.4 At the fork, stay right. From here the trail crosses the creek several times. Always stay on the main trail.

5.0 Just after a creek crossing you encounter a road going both left and right. Turn right here and begin a pleasant cruise up and through the trees. (**Note:** If going to Croy Creek from here, turn left to the Kelly Mountain saddle at the top. Use common sense in directions going down the other side. It's approximately 4.5 miles to Croy Creek Road and 16 miles into Hailey. Use USGS topographical map "Mahoney Butte" and "Richardson Butte.")

5.4 After crossing a small creek, continue up the main road. Do not turn left on the faint singletrack. From here the road is a bit steep and loose.

6.3 The first of many saddles is reached. Follow the road down a bit before starting some serious climbing.

6.8 The road takes a sharp right turn and becomes singletrack climbing up to the left. You may have to push a bit here, but hang in there. It mellows in a bit before traversing over to the saddle above Kinsey Creek.

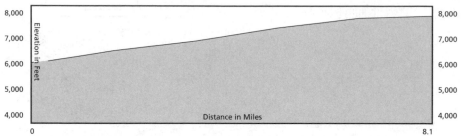

8.1 The saddle on top of Kinsey Creek. Drop into Kinsey Creek to end this ride. Or you may continue on into Curran Gulch—the details of this ride are listed under the Kinsey Creek to Curran Gulch.

13 Kinsey Creek to Curran Gulch

This isn't as bad as the elevation gain seems, but it is still a grinder. Once up, it's a great run down. Fairly sandy on the way up and technical on the way down.

Distance: 10.4 miles
Difficulty rating: Difficult
Technical rating: 3+
The ride: Loop
Starting elevation: 6,040 feet
High point elevation: 7,800 feet

Total elevation gain: 1,760 feet
Surface: Dirt jeep road and singletrack trail
Season: Early June through October
Fun factor: Adventure ride, views, route-finding, views, route . . .

Getting there: From Ketchum, drive south on Highway 75 for approximately 9 miles and turn right at the forest service sign for DEER CREEK ROAD. Follow this road for 11.5 miles and park next to the unsigned Kinsey Creek coming into the canyon from the left. There are big boulders here to prevent you from driving across the creek. Park somewhere nearby, but please don't block the road.

Miles and Directions

0.0 Begin by riding through Deer Creek then up the trail into the Kinsey Creek drainage.

1.2 Pass by a trail leading off to the right, which eventually leads into the Curran Gulch drainage. Stay on the main trail passing a spur road on the left.

1.5 At the fork in the road, take the left and more heavily traveled road that crosses the creek. From here you begin a long climb.

3.5 The top of the saddle. From here the trail gets a bit more interesting. Straight ahead leads into Croy Creek and left leads to Wolftone Creek. Instead, turn right at the top of the saddle and ride for roughly 50+ feet on a primitive trail, before jumping off to the left on a trail that descends quickly to a road about 50 yards below. Yes, it is the trail if you go literally straight down the hill. Turn right onto the road and follow it for one mile, where it starts to switchback to the right and climb.

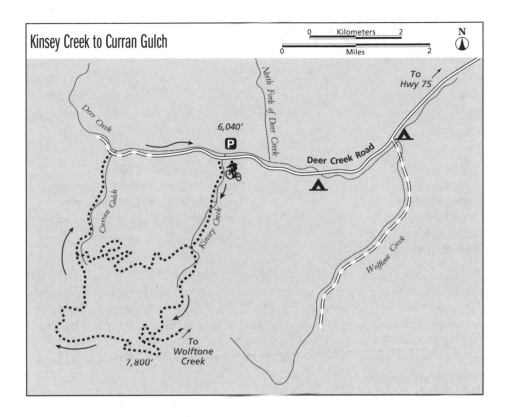

Kinsey Creek to Curran Gulch

4.5 After rounding the switchback, continue for a couple hundred yards. Look to your left for a trail leading off to the left traversing the ridge. (**Note:** DO NOT MISS THIS TURN.)

5.5 After gaining the final ridge-top, the trail becomes a bit of a roller-coaster as it drops its way into Curran Gulch.

7.3 You'll come to a trail junction with a trail coming in from Kinsey Creek. Stay straight and continue down the drainage.

8.8 After crossing over Deer Creek, meet up with the Deer Creek Trail and turn right, heading down the drainage.

9.8 Ride past the official trailhead for the Deer Creek Trail and enter into a hunters camp and onto a dirt jeep road. Continue down the road.

10.4 The end of the ride and back at the Kinsey Creek trailhead.

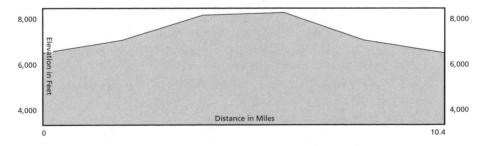

14 Quigley Creek to Cove Creek

Whether you shuttle a car to Triumph or make a loop out of it, this is a wonderful ride for most anyone. Due to the length, it will leave you with a good thigh burn. High alpine meadows, aspens, and the occasional elk or antelope just add to the experience.

Distance: 31.1 miles
Difficulty rating: Moderate/Difficult
Technical rating: 2
The ride: Loop
Starting elevation: 5,350 feet
High point elevation: 7,250 feet

Total elevation gain: 1,900 feet
Surface: Dirt road, singletrack, pavement
Season: Late April through late October
Fun factor: Pioneer mountain views, wildlife, and solitude

Getting there: From the stoplight at Bullion Street and Highway 75 in downtown Hailey, drive one block south to Croy Street and turn left here. After 0.5 mile, follow the road around a natural right turn and take an immediate left onto Quigley Gulch Road, which is directly in front of the DEERFIELD sign. Continue forward to where the pavement turns to dirt and park here. (**Note:** You can ride on singletrack for quite a ways up Quigley right from the parking area. The singletrack parallels the road just past the parking area on the left and ends at the cattle guard by the pond, then starts up again to the right, just after the fence by the pond and goes to the corrals. Don't miss out on this fun part of the canyon!)

Miles and Directions

0.0 Begin riding up Quigley Gulch heading east alongside a large field and across the cattle guard.

1.75 Pass Quigley Pond on the right side of the road.

2.2 Small spur road on the right. Continue straight on Quigley Gulch.

2.5 The spur road rejoins the main road.

4.2 Pass a corral then a spur road just a bit further on the left side.

5.8 Spur road on the left leads to/from Indian Creek. Continue up the main road curving to the south up and through some clear cuts. Always stay on the main road through this area.

7.6 Small private cabin appears off to the right.

7.7 Spur road and switchback leads off to the right, which heads over and down to Slaughterhouse Creek and into Bellevue. Stay on the main road crossing over a small creek bed (possibly dry in mid to late summer) and heading northeast.

8.6 Saddle in a mud-bog area. Take the first left heading down the canyon to the northeast and left. Do not turn right; it leads nowhere.

9.1 After a bit of a rutted downhill, a road takes off to the left just before a muddy creek crossing. Stay on the main road through the muddy crossing.

9.4 Take a left on the grassy doubletrack . . . trust me.

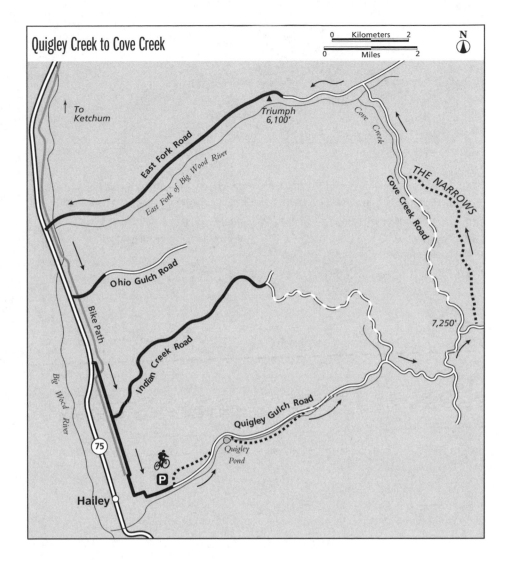

Quigley Creek to Cove Creek

10.1 Take another left and go down the hill.

10.4 Yes, go left again and begin the famous, singletrack Narrows Trail.

11.7 The Narrows ends at Cove Creek Road. Go right and toward the beaver ponds, heading north.

12.6 A fun descent leads to a junction with another main road. Go right here passing by the beaver ponds and a spur road on the right. Continue down the main road.

13.7 Pass by Hook Draw on the right.

14.2 Small spur road on the left leads to nowhere.

16.2 Major junction here. This is East Fork Road. Turn left here.

17.2 Spur road off to the right leads to Hyndman Creek and the Pioneer Mountains main "peak" district.

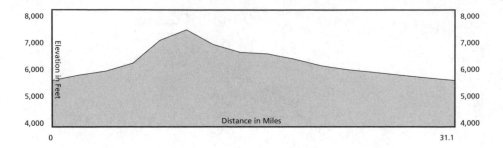

18.5 Pavement and the town of Triumph. If you shuttled a car here, this is the end of your ride. If you're bumming that there's no car here, continue down the paved East Fork Road.

24.4 Turn left before Highway 75 and head south on the paved bike path.

30.6 As the bike path comes into Hailey, follow it to Croy Street and turn left here, retracing your route back to your car.

31.1 Back at your car at Quigley Canyon and the end of the ride.

Riding around the Ketchum Area

Mountain biking around Ketchum over the past ten years has become a mecca for enthusiasts, coming from both far and wide. The area is not spoken about in terms of a Moab or Fruita, as most people who come to Ketchum don't like to tell others of their find. Once you've ridden around Ketchum, undoubtedly you'll be coming back for your pilgrimage to mecca year after year.

The trails here have been compared to a smooth brown carpet surrounded by pine trees. We even heard one visitor from out of state say, "I heard that everyone gets together in Ketchum and sweeps the trails." Yes, the trails are smooth and velvety, but not THAT smooth and velvety, so don't expect a miracle, but you will be impressed.

Most visitors to the area tend to congregate at the Adams Gulch Area, due to its proximity to Ketchum, as do the lunchtime locals needing their "hour of power." However, there are SO many other places to go play around the immediate area that are equal, if not better, including Greenhorn Gulch Area, Deer Creek Area, Galena Lodge Area, and Bald Mountain (on the latter, you can either ride the lift up and just do a downhill, or ride up and down on the trails—either way is a blast).

Regardless of where you ride around the area, you're sure to have a smile on your face at the end of the day. Don't be afraid to ask other riders questions or suggestions for other trails to ride, as most everyone is friendly and will offer great advice.

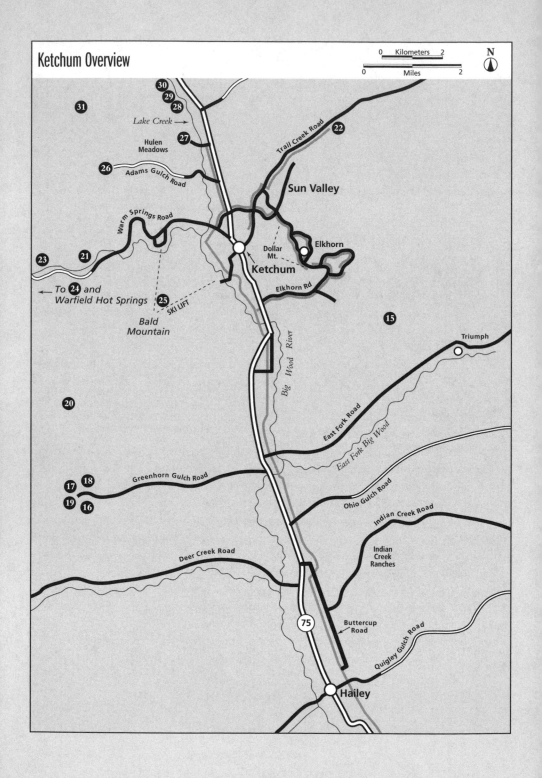

Ketchum Overview

Kilometers 0 — 2
Miles 0 — 2

N

30
29
28
31

Lake Creek →

27

Hulen
Meadows

Trail Creek Road

22

26

Adams Gulch Road

Sun Valley

Warm Springs Road

Dollar
Mt.

Elkhorn

23   **21**

Ketchum

15

← To **24** and
Warfield Hot Springs

25

SKI LIFT

Elkhorn Rd

Triumph

*Bald
Mountain*

Big Wood River

East Fork Road

20

East Fork Big Wood

Greenhorn Gulch Road

17   **18**

19   **16**

Ohio Gulch Road

Indian Creek Road

Indian
Creek
Ranches

Deer Creek Road

75

Buttercup
Road →

Quigley Gulch Road

Hailey

15 Parker to Bear Gulch Loop

You'll burn your lungs and pound your legs, all for the most amazing views and wildlife everywhere! This is a must-do ride if ya think ya can handle it!

Distance: 20.8 miles
Difficulty rating: Difficult
Technical rating: 3 (mainly going up Parker)
The ride: Loop
Starting elevation: 6,005 feet
High point elevation: 8,610 feet

Total elevation gain: 2,605 feet
Surface: Dirt jeep road and singletrack
Season: Late May through October
Fun factor: Pioneer Mountain views like you've never seen before

Getting there: From Ketchum, drive south on Highway 75 to East Fork Road, approximately 5 miles. Turn left (east) here and drive approximately 5 miles and park on the left where a major dirt jeep road takes off. This is where the ride begins. If you went to Triumph, turn around 1 mile to the starting point.

Miles and Directions

0.0 Begin by riding up Triumph Gulch on a fairly major jeep road.

1.5 At the fork, stay left.

2.9 Round a saddle with views of Elkhorn and the valley below.

4.2 Go screaming by Independence Mine. DO NOT GO INTO ANY SHAFTS!

5.5 Jeep road ends at pavement above The Ranch at Elkhorn condos.

6.1 At the stop sign, go right.

6.7 Again, at the stop sign, go right. This is the beginning of Parker Gulch Road.

8.5 The gravel road now becomes doubletrack jeep road.

9.4 In the big grassy meadow, stay left and you'll find the trail again. It is singletrack from here on up.

9.9 The switchbacks begin. Now is when you need those lungs and legs!

11.4 The first saddle, hold on, there's more . . .

12.0 The top of the ride at 8,610 feet, overlooking Uncle John's Gulch to the north and Bear Gulch to the south. To the east are the Pioneer Mountains.

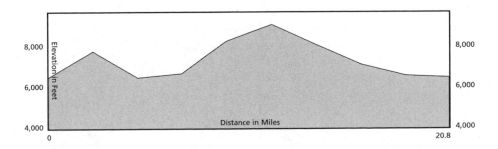

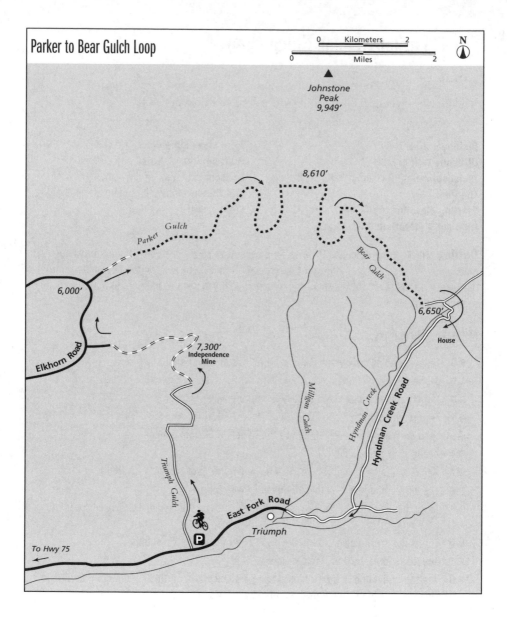

Parker to Bear Gulch Loop

0 Kilometers **2**
0 Miles **2**

N

Johnstone
Peak
9,949'

8,610'

Parker Gulch

6,000'

Bear Gulch

6,650'

House

Elkhorn Road

7,300'
**Independence
Mine**

Milligan Gulch

Hyndman Creek

Hyndman Creek Road

Triumph Gulch

East Fork Road

Triumph

P

To Hwy 75

12.5 A small saddle before really dropping into Bear Gulch. Stay left at the fork.

15.5 Singletrack ends at a doubletrack jeep road.

15.7 Junction with Hyndman Creek Road; stay right and down. You'll follow this all the way down the valley.

18.6 Take a right onto East Fork Road.

19.8 The town of Triumph. Watch for kids and cruise through town.

20.8 The end of the ride and back at your car (on the right!).

16 Imperial Gulch

With a grind up Greenhorn Gulch, you are rewarded with a great descent into Imperial Gulch with views, flowers, wildlife, and more views.

Distance: 10.5 miles
Difficulty rating: Moderate/Difficult
Technical rating: 2+
The ride: Loop
Starting elevation: 5,900 feet
High point elevation: 7,450 feet

Total elevation gain: 1,550 feet
Surface: Singletrack trail
Season: May through October
Fun factor: Scenic, fun loop and incredible downhill

Getting there: From Ketchum, drive south on Highway 75 for 6 miles and turn right (west) at the light onto Greenhorn Gulch Road. Follow the road through Golden Eagle Subdivision to the end of the road, and follow the dirt road for 0.5 mile to the parking lot. The ride begins here.

Miles and Directions

0.0 Follow the trail exiting the parking lot area on the west side. The beginning of this trail is quite rocky and rough, but don't let this turn you off; it's great at the top.

(Alternative Better Start: Exit the parking lot and head down the small hill to the south and cross the creek. Just after going up a small hill through the aspens, take a small spur trail to the right and stay next to the creek along the bench. The trail intersects the junction below at 1.4 miles. This start will also put your mileage off by about 0.2 mile.)

1.0 Pass by Cow Creek Trail on the right.

1.4 Trail junction. Right trail leads to Mahoney Creek and Lodgepole Gulch, but turn left and continue up toward Deer Creek, gradually climbing through pines next to the stream.

3.8 You see an unsigned trail on the right that leads up Mahoney Creek, but continue straight on the main trail heading toward Deer Creek with casual climbing through beautiful pines alongside the creek.

4.9 You encounter a trail junction at the saddle. From here take a hard left, passing by a trail exiting off to the right and down into Deer Creek. This is the beginning of Imperial Gulch Trail. For the next 2.7 miles the trail traverses with minimal climbing giving wonderful views of Deer Creek and the Mahoney Creek drainages.

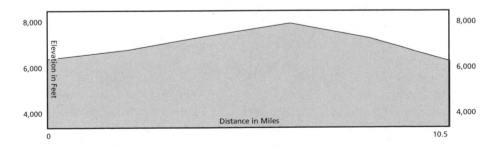

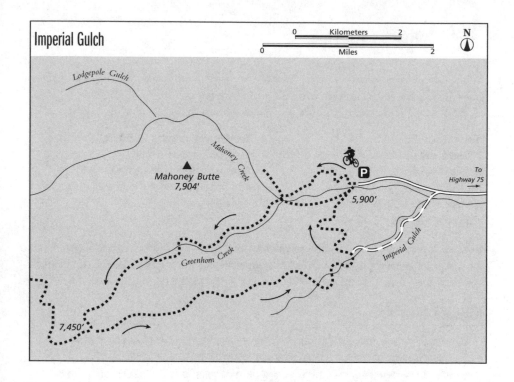

7.6 Whoa! Be sure and turn right here where the sign indicates TRAIL.

8.1 Faint trail leading off to the right leads into Deer Creek. Stay straight on the main trail heading down the gulch.

8.8 Trail junction at the fence. The right trail leads to another Imperial Gulch trailhead. Instead, turn left, traversing gradually up and to a saddle overlooking Greenhorn Gulch.

9.3 The saddle. Continue on down the trail.

10.3 The bottom of Imperial Gulch Trail at the intersection with Greenhorn Gulch. Turn right and continue back to the trailhead.

10.5 The end of the ride and back at the trailhead.

17 Lodgepole Gulch

This whole area is a great place for riding, no matter which loop you do. Lodgepole Gulch is known for its great downhills and moderate climbs.

Distance: 11.9 miles
Difficulty rating: Moderate/Difficult
Technical rating: 2
The ride: Loop
Starting elevation: 5,900 feet
High point elevation: 7,850 feet

Total elevation gain: 1,950 feet
Surface: singletrack trail
Season: May through late October
Fun factor: Wildflowers, climbing, great downhill, meadows

Getting there: From Ketchum, drive south on Highway 75 for 6 miles and turn right (west) at the light onto Greenhorn Gulch Road. Follow the road through Golden Eagle Subdivision to the end of the road, and follow the dirt road for 0.5 mile to the parking lot. The ride begins here.

Miles and Directions

0.0 Follow the trail exiting the parking lot area on the west side. The beginning of this trail is quite rocky and rough, but don't let this turn you off.

(Alternative Better Start: Exit the parking lot and head down the small hill to the south and cross the creek. Just after going up a small hill through the aspens, take a small spur trail to the right and stay next to the creek along the bench. The trail intersects the junction below at 1.4 miles. This start will also put your mileage off by about 0.2 mile.)

1.0 Pass by Cow Creek Trail on the right.

1.4 Trail junction. Turn right toward Mahoney Creek Trail and Lodgepole Trail and begin a gradual ascent.

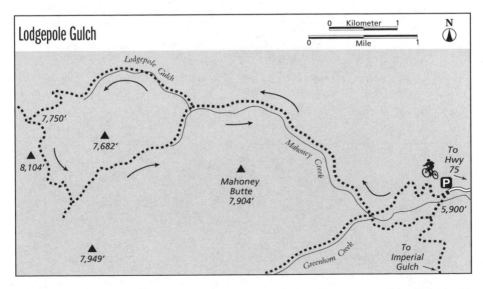

You're never too young to enjoy the ride.

3.7 You reach a trail junction. Turn right and into Lodgepole Gulch. From here you climb about 1,000 feet over the next 2.1 miles. It is never too hard, so take many deep breaths, endure the grind, and relax and enjoy the beautiful scenery.

5.8 Trail junction at the top of Lodgepole Gulch. Turn left and begin descending down into Mahoney Creek. The right trail leads into Red Warrior Creek.

6.7 Trail junction. The right fork leads to the top of Mahoney Creek; instead, turn left and down, the drainage.

8.4 Trail junction. The left fork leads back up into Lodgepole Gulch, instead, turn right and down heading back to the trailhead.

10.5 Trail junction. The right fork leads up Greenhorn Creek and into Deer Creek. Instead, turn left to complete the loop.

11.9 Back at the trailhead and the end of the ride.

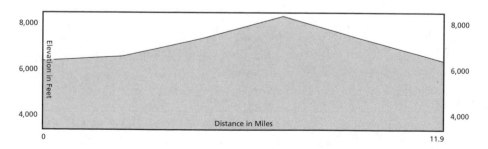

18 Cow Creek Loop

This whole area is a great place for riding, no matter which loop you do. Cow Creek is still a bit of a primitive trail compared to the other trails in the area. Be prepared for a little bit of adventure.

Distance: 8.4 miles
Difficulty rating: Moderate/Difficult
Technical rating: 2+
The ride: Loop
Starting elevation: 5,900 feet
High point elevation: 6,900 feet

Total elevation gain: 1,000 feet
Surface: Singletrack trail
Season: May through late October
Fun factor: Wildflowers, climbing, great downhill, meadows

Getting there: From Ketchum, drive south on Highway 75 for 6 miles and turn right (west) at the light onto Greenhorn Gulch Road. Follow the road through Golden Eagle Subdivision to the end of the road, and follow the dirt road for 0.5 mile to the parking lot. The ride begins here.

Miles and Directions

0.0 Follow the trail exiting the parking lot area on the west side. The beginning of this trail is quite rocky and rough, but don't let this turn you off.

(Alternative Better Start: Exit the parking lot and head down the small hill to the south and cross the creek. Just after going up a small hill through the aspens, take a small spur trail to the right and stay next to the creek along the bench. The trail intersects the junction below at 1.4 miles. This start will also put your mileage off by about 0.2 mile.)

1.0 Pass by Cow Creek Trail on the right. This is where you'll come out.

1.4 Trail junction. Turn right toward Mahoney Creek Trail and Lodgepole Gulch and begin a gradual ascent.

3.7 You reach a trail junction. Turn right and into Lodgepole Gulch. After about 200 feet, look right and follow a faint trail that begins to climb up and northeast. Be sure you're on the correct trail (second right), as there is an old trail just before the correct one. But remember, these are very faint trails. You'll follow this trail as it roller-coasters and contours along the hillsides to a nice big pond and boggy area.

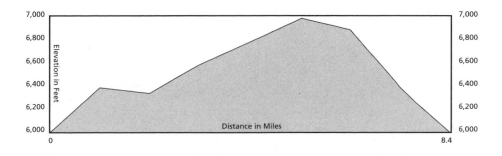

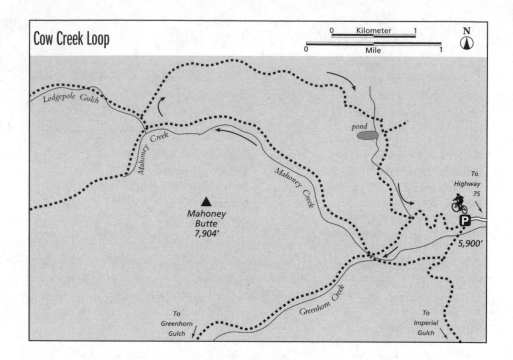

Cow Creek Loop

5.4 The big pond and boggy area. At the far end of the wet area (east end), be sure to curve around to the south, bypassing a faint trail that peels off to the left and over a small saddle. That faint trail is a bit more adventurous as it gets lost in a log area before turning to serious boulder-hopping and the parking lot. Instead, stay on the trail heading south and down.

7.0 Trail junction. Look familiar? That's right, you were here once before on your way out on the start. Turn left and head back up and over to the parking lot.

8.4 The parking lot and back at your car.

19 Greenhorn Gulch to Mahoney Creek

This ride is always an aerobic challenge with wonderful singletrack trails, views of the Pioneer Mountains, and some of the best downhill riding around.

Distance: 12.8 miles
Difficulty rating: Difficult
Technical rating: 2+
The ride: Loop
Starting elevation: 5,900 feet
High point elevation: 8,000 feet

Total elevation gain: 2,100 feet
Surface: Singletrack trail
Season: May through late October
Fun factor: Moderate climbs leading to excellent views and downhills

Getting there: From Ketchum, drive south on Highway 75 for 6 miles and turn right (west) at the light onto Greenhorn Gulch Road. Follow the road through Golden Eagle Subdivision to the end of the road, and follow the dirt road for 0.5 mile to the parking lot. The ride begins here.

Miles and Directions

0.0 Follow the trail exiting the parking lot area on the west side. The beginning of this trail is quite rocky and rough, but don't let this turn you off.

(Alternative Better Start: Exit the parking lot and head down the small hill to the south and cross the creek. Just after going up a small hill through the aspens, take a small spur trail to the right and stay next to the creek along the bench. The trail intersects the junction below at 1.4 miles. This start will also put your mileage off by about 0.2 mile.)

1.0 Pass by Cow Creek Trail on the right.

1.4 Trail junction: Right trail leads to Mahoney Creek and Lodgepole Gulch, but turn left and continue up toward Deer Creek, ascending the trail through pines next to a stream.

3.8 An unsigned trail on the right leads up Mahoney Creek. Continue straight on the main trail heading toward Deer Creek.

4.9 Catch your breath at the trail junction midway through the climb. Hard left eventually leads to Imperial Gulch Trail 155, while a soft left leads down a jeep trail to Deer Creek via Panther Creek. Instead, continue grinding up and right on Mahoney Creek Trail 156 climbing a few switchbacks and eventually gaining the top of the ride with incredible views of the Pioneer Mountains to the east.

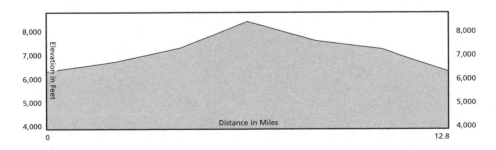

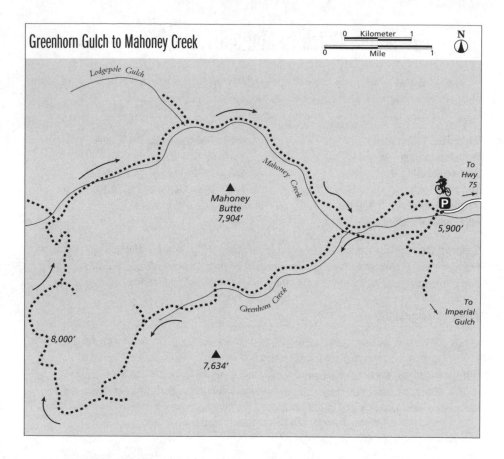

Greenhorn Gulch to Mahoney Creek

Lodgepole Gulch

Mahoney Creek

Mahoney Butte 7,904'

To Hwy 75

5,900'

To Imperial Gulch

Greenhorn Creek

8,000'

7,634'

6.6 After a few roller-coasters, you come to a trail junction. Left trail leads down Red Warrior Creek Trail 152, but continue down right on the main trail, eventually passing by the unsigned Mahoney Creek Trail in a saddle on the right side after 0.5 mile.

7.6 Trail junction. Left trail leads into Lodgepole Gulch. Instead, continue down and right on the main trail through a wonderful tree slalom course. Please remember your trail etiquette here: no skidding and yield to all others.

9.1 Trail junction. Left trail leads up Lodgepole Gulch. Continue the ride down on the main trail. Watch that smile; you may have to pick a few bugs out of your teeth.

11.4 The loop is complete. Continue left and down, crossing the stream two more times, the same way you came up.

12.8 The parking lot and the end of the ride.

20 Red Warrior Creek

A ride up Lodgepole Gulch leads to a great technical descent through creeks and rocks to a huge creek crossing and hot springs. Views abound in every direction.

Distance: 10.7 miles (30.2 miles for loop)
Difficulty rating: Difficult
Technical rating: 3+
The ride: One-way or loop option
Starting elevation: 5,900 feet
High point elevation: 7,850 feet

Total elevation gain: 1,950 feet
Surface: singletrack trail and dirt jeep road
Season: May through late October
Fun factor: Great climbing, killer descent, and hot springs

Getting there: From Ketchum, drive south on Highway 75 for 6 miles and turn right (west) onto Greenhorn Gulch Road. Drive 3.8 miles up the road to the parking lot. The ride begins here. (**Note:** You may want to shuttle a car up Warm Springs Road to the end of the ride at Warfield Hot Springs, or plan on enjoying the casual ride back down Warm Springs Road into Ketchum and back to the trailhead—approximately 20 miles).

Miles and Directions

0.0 Follow the trail exiting the parking lot area on the west side. The trail is quite rocky and rough, but don't let this turn you off; it's great at the top.

(**Alternative Better Start:** Exit the parking lot and head down the small hill to the south and cross the creek. Just after going up a small hill through the aspens, take a small spur trail to the right and stay next to the creek along the bench. The trail intersects the junction below at 1.4 miles. This start will also put your mileage off by about 0.2 mile.)

1.0 Pass by Cow Creek Trail on the right.

1.4 Trail junction. Turn right toward Mahoney Creek Trail and Lodgepole Gulch and begin a gradual ascent.

3.7 You reach a trail junction. Turn right and into Lodgepole Gulch. From here you climb about 1,000 feet over the next 2.1 miles. It is never too hard, so take many deep breaths, endure the grind, and relax and enjoy the beautiful scenery.

5.8 At the next trail junction, turn right heading up and over into Red Warrior Creek. The left fork here drops down into Mahoney Creek.

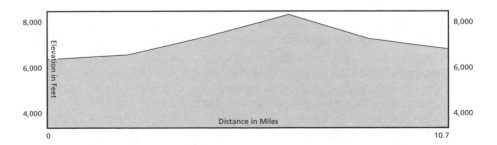

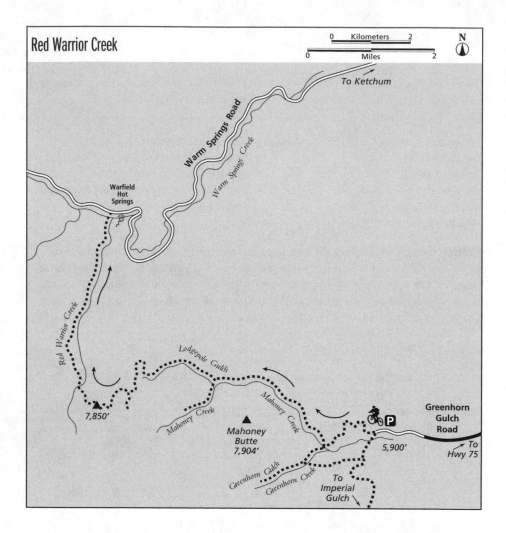

Kilometers

Miles

N

To Ketchum

Warm Springs Road

Warm Springs Creek

Warfield Hot Springs

Red Warrior Creek

Lodgepole Gulch

7,850'

Mahoney Creek

Mahoney Creek

Mahoney Butte 7,904'

Greenhorn Gulch

Greenhorn Creek

5,900'

Greenhorn Gulch Road

To Hwy 75

To Imperial Gulch

6.1 At the saddle between Lodgepole Gulch and Red Warrior Creek, you begin some fast descending switchbacks for the next 1.2 miles. Once at the bottom and into the Red Warrior Creek drainage, prepare to get wet. You'll cross the creek anywhere between sixteen and twenty-four times, depending upon the time of year and dryness of the upper creek.

8.3 Continuing forward, you'll pass by a trail leading up and to the left. That trail eventually joins up to Mars Ridge.

9.2 Prepare for a gnarly descent. Soon you'll notice an old metal shack and from here the trail crosses the creek eight times while the trail winds its way down the drainage.

10.7 The climax of the ride . . . crossing over Warm Springs Creek. No, there is not a bridge, so get wet and enjoy it. This is the end of the ride if you shuttled a car to this point. Warm Springs Road is right in front of you, as are about three hot springs next to the creek a couple hundred yards down the road. Turn right, and from here it is approximately 10 miles back to Ketchum, and an additional 10 miles back to the Greenhorn Gulch trailhead, all gradually descending.

21 Corral Creek

This ride has it all, quick climbs (never too steep), quick turns in a slalom fashion, and one of the best downhills this close to Ketchum.

Distance: 6.8 miles
Difficulty: Easy/Moderate
Technical rating: 1
The ride: Out-and-back
Starting elevation: 6,075 feet
High point: 6,750 feet

Total elevation gain: 675 feet
Surface: Singletrack trail
Season: Late April through late October
Fun factor: Sagebrush slalom courses with incredible downhills

Getting there: From Ketchum, drive east on Sun Valley/Trail Creek Road for 3.7 miles, passing by Trail Creek Cabin along the way. Turn right where the sign points to Trail Creek trailhead, just past the Boundary Campground. Be sure to park in the trailhead parking lot (day use) and NOT the picnic or campground areas. The ride begins here.

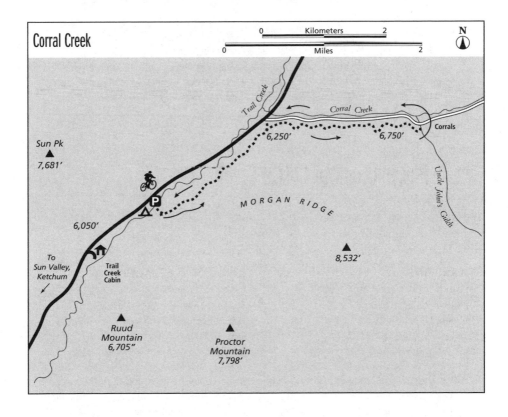

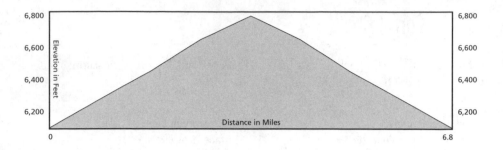

Miles and Directions

0.0 Begin by riding along the gravel trail (upstream and east) to the wooden bridge and cross it. Follow this trail up the embankment and across the sagebrush flats to the trail junction.

0.1 Trail junction. Turn left and follow the singletrack trail along the foothills heading up the valley. Remember to stay on singletrack the entire time, since you will be crossing a few faint jeep roads along the way.

1.4 Whoa! Trail junction. Stay to the right on the main trail. The left fork leads down to Trail Creek Road.

2.9 Junction with a jeep road crossing. Simply cross the road and keep cruising!

3.4 Take a minute, unpack your lunch, or just enjoy Uncle John's Gulch and the sheep corrals. From here, turn around and get ready for the best ride of your life. (**FYI:** A great alternative ride from here is to ride up Uncle John's Gulch for a couple more miles of fairly mellow climbing and an even better downhill back to Corral Creek Trail.)

6.8 Return to Trail Creek trailhead parking lot and end of the ride.

22 Placer Creek to Castle Creek

If you can get by the loose rock and pushing for a little ways on the way up, you'll dig the downhill all the way back to your car.

Distance: 10.9 miles
Difficulty rating: Moderate/Difficult
Technical rating: 3+
The ride: Loop
Starting elevation: 6,640 feet
High point elevation: 8,220 feet

Total elevation gain: 1,580 feet
Surface: Dirt jeep road and singletrack
Season: Late May through October
Fun factor: Adventure and the feeling of being way out there

Getting there: From Ketchum, drive north on Highway 75 for 3 blocks and turn left at the light onto Warm Springs Road. Follow this road for approximately 15.5 miles and park on the left just after the trailhead sign for Castle Creek. You'll know you're there when a big castle-like rock appears on the north side of the creek (right side). This is where the ride begins.

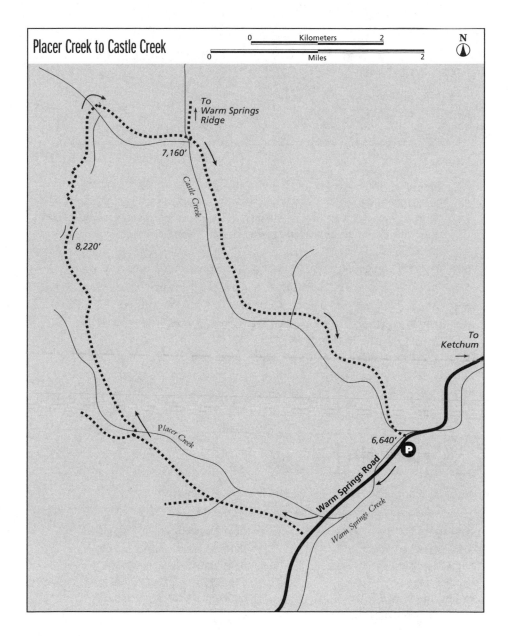

Miles and Directions

0.0 Begin by riding up Warm Springs Road to the turn-off for Placer Creek.

1.3 Turn right on the jeep road next to the corrals. Stay on this main road.

2.3 Cross the obvious creek in front of you.

3.0 Another creek crossing . . . enjoy the wetness!

3.1 This rough road leads to a small sign on the right. Follow the trail to the right.

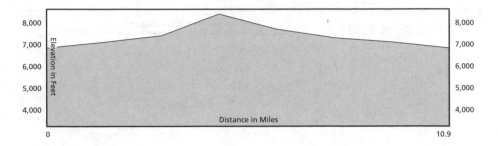

4.8 Stay on the main trail here.

5.0 The trail starts to level out a bit and then hits a very marshy area. It's not that bad, and the upper end of the water-crested stream has some small logs on which to cross. From here, follow the trail through the forest, where it goes through numerous springs and over logs. Eventually it dries out.

5.5 The top of the ride. Get ready for the most amazing downhill. Be careful!

6.6 After some serious switchbacks, you cross over Castle Creek. Go right.

8.3 Cross over the North Fork of Castle Creek. Look upstream for a crossing.

9.5 The trail goes through a huge meadow and disappears. Stay straight through the meadow. The trail reappears at the other end.

10.7 Cross through Castle Creek. Get wet; you're almost done!

10.8 Cross through Warm Springs Creek. Keep trying until you get it. Get wet!

10.9 After crossing Warm Springs Creek, turn right on the road and return to your car.

23 Poison Flat Trail

Moderate climbing, great views, and incredible downhills.

Distance: 13.2 miles
Difficulty rating: Difficult
Technical rating: 2+
The ride: One-way
Starting elevation: 6,850 feet
High point elevation: 7,900 feet

Total elevation gain: 1,050 feet
Surface: Dirt jeep road and singletrack trail
Season: Late May through late October
Fun factor: Wildflowers, high alpine meadows, cruiser downhills

Getting there: From the heart of Ketchum, drive north on Highway 75 for 3 blocks and turn left onto Warm Springs Road. Follow this road up Warm Springs Canyon approximately 18 miles where a pull-out on the left shows signs for Road 046 (South and Middle Forks of Warm Springs Creek). Park anywhere near here. You will need to shuttle a car to the North Fork of Deer Creek parking area (see the North Fork of Deer Creek ride on page 31 for directions).

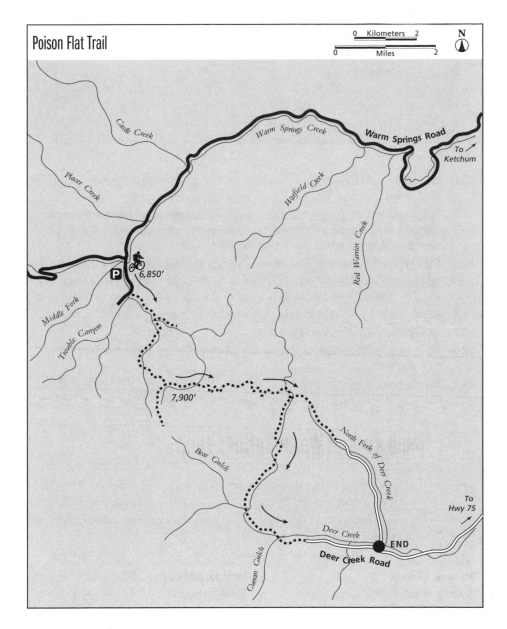

Poison Flat Trail

Miles and Directions

0.0 Begin by riding up South Fork of Warm Springs 046 in a southerly direction on a partial jeep road, immediately forging a stream.

0.7 Turn left at the sign for Meadow Creek Trail and cross the creek.

1.0 Again, turn left at the sign for South Fork of Warm Springs Trail 151.

2.4 Trail junction. The left fork goes up to Red Warrior Creek. Instead, go right and continue up South Fork of Warm Springs Trail 199.

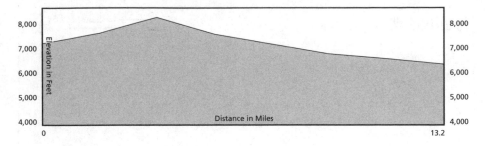

3.1 The trail turns into a tough climb through loose scree for only a short distance, gaining a small saddle soon thereafter.

4.3 Trail junction. Do not go right, it is a very challenging trail that could involve a few tears and hair-pulling. Instead, save the marriage and turn left onto Poison Flat Trail 218 and begin a scenic cruise across the high alpine sage-brush meadow.

6.6 Trail junction. The left fork goes up and over into the North Fork of Deer Creek. Take the right fork into the main drainage of Deer Creek. However, either trail will get you back to your (shuttled) car at the trailhead.

8.7 As you descend, pass by Horn Creek on the right; Bear Gulch is a mile later.

10.7 Pass by Curran Gulch on the right side.

12.0 The trailhead for Deer Creek Trail and a primitive hunters' camp. Continue on down the main jeep road.

13.2 The end of the ride.

24 South Fork of Warm Springs Loop

You'll feel like you're way out in the wilderness with no one else around. This transforms from a dirt jeep road to an ATV trail to a singletrack trail to complete the loop. Be ready for great climbing (all rideable) and some great descents that'll make your forearms whimper for a break!

Distance: 11 miles

Difficulty rating: Moderate

Technical rating: 2

The ride: Loop

Starting elevation: 6,840 feet

High point elevation: 8,800 feet

Total elevation gain: 2,040 feet

Surface: Dirt jeep road, ATV trail, singletrack trail

Season: May through late October

Fun factor: Amazing views over Dollarhide Summit, wildlife, and an incredible trail

Getting there: From the heart of Ketchum, drive north on Highway 75 for 3 blocks and turn left onto Warm Springs Road. Follow this road up Warm Springs Canyon approximately 18 miles where a pull-out on the left shows signs for Road 046 (South and Middle Forks of Warm Springs Creek). Park anywhere near here.

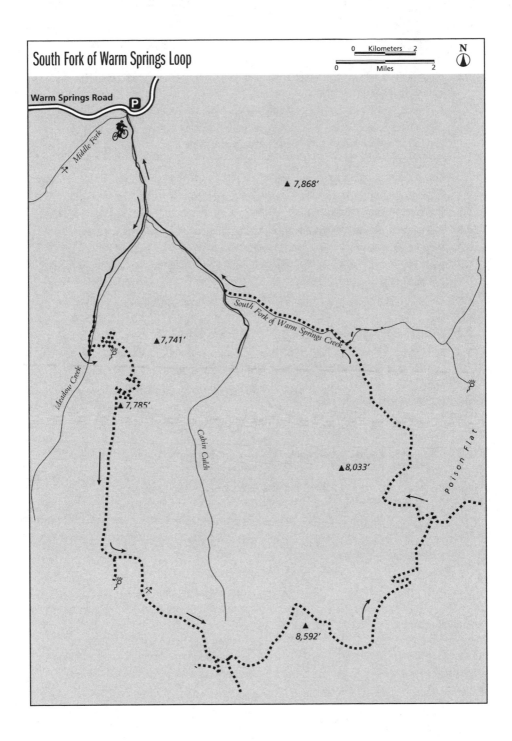

South Fork of Warm Springs Loop

Kilometers 0 — 2

Miles 0 — 2

N

Warm Springs Road

Middle Fork

▲ 7,868'

South Fork of Warm Springs Creek

▲ 7,741'

Meadow Creek

▲ 7,785'

Cabin Gulch

▲ 8,033'

Poison Flat

▲ 8,592'

Miles and Directions

0.0   Begin riding across Warm Springs Creek and then again over the South Fork of Warm Springs Creek shortly thereafter.

0.7   Trail junction in a meadow. Veer right and head up Meadow Creek.

1.8   You'll reach a meadow where the jeep road ends; just look left and down by the creek and you'll see the start of the ATV trail heading across the creek and up the hills to the east of you.

3.8   After a series of switchbacks, you gain a nice open ridge and can see your destiny ahead of you . . .

4.6   Trail junction. Stay left here even though you'll meet up with that other trail again shortly.

4.9   Trail junction. Stay left here again after passing some mines and mining ruins.

5.3   On a flat section, you'll pass by some pioneer cabin ruins on the left.

5.7   Trail junction. Stay left on the main trail here, then at the next junction, stay uphill or right just before the singletrack start.

5.8   The start of the singletrack on the left. Follow this as it contours down towards Poison Flat.

6.7   You start a series of switchbacks that are quite rocky . . . hope you have a "bouncy bike" !

7.4   Trail junction with Poison Flat Trail. Take a left and go downhill all the way back to your car! The right trail would take you over Poison Flat to the North Fork of Deer Creek.

8.5   Trail junction. Stay left or down the drainage. The trail to the right would lead overland to Red Warrior Creek (very rough!).

9.5   Trail junction with a jeep road. Stay to the right and head down the jeep trail back towards your car.

10.3   Back in the meadow that you left behind 10 miles and several power gels earlier. Take a right.

11.0   The end of the ride and back at your car. Nice job! Feels good, doesn't it?!

25 Bald Mountain Trails

There are a plethora of trails on Bald Mountain, and the best part is its proximity to Ketchum. If you want to go big, ride power, or just get an aerobic fix, this is a great place to go. The River Run parking lot is a great meeting place to start any of the rides. Here are some options:

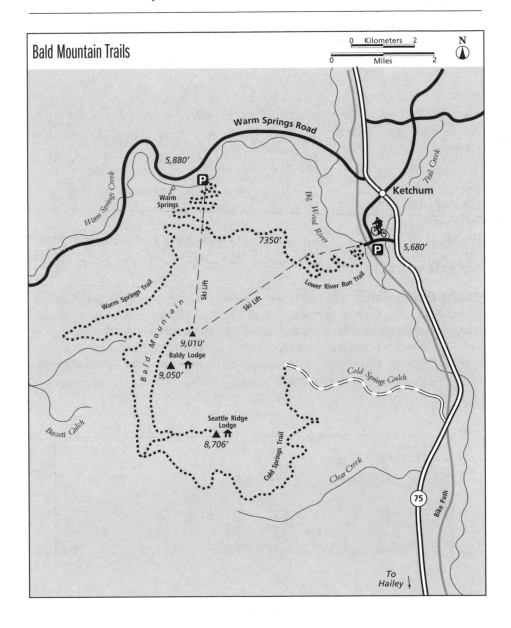

Bald Mountain Trails

0 Kilometers 2

0 Miles 2

N

Warm Springs Road

5,880'

Warm Springs Creek

P

Warm Springs

Trail Creek

Ketchum

Big Wood River

7350'

P

5,680'

Warm Springs Trail

Ski Lift

Ski Lift

Lower River Run Trail

Bald Mountain

9,010'

Baldy Lodge

9,050'

Cold Springs Gulch

Bassett Gulch

Seattle Ridge Lodge

8,706'

Cold Springs Trail

Clear Creek

75

Bike Path

To Hailey

1. **BIG ride:** Go up Warm Springs, down Cold Springs, and back to River Run.

2. **Aerobic ride:** Go up Bald Mountain hiking trail (from River Run), then back down Lower River Run.

3. **Classic loop:** Lower River Run Trail to Warm Springs and back through town to the River Run parking lot.

4. **Downhiller:** Ride the lift up River Run and descend Warm Springs, Cold Springs, and/or Lower River Run. Be careful of the uphill riders!

25a Warm Springs Trail

If you're riding up the trail, it gradually climbs and switchbacks most of the way up this side of the mountain before gaining a ridge and winding its way to the top via the west side of the mountain. If you're riding down, be cautious of other riders and hikers moving in your opposite direction.

Distance: 9.1 miles
Difficulty rating: Moderate
Technical rating: 1
The ride: One-way
Starting elevation: 9,010 feet
Ending elevation: 5,880 feet

Total elevation gain/loss: 3,130 feet
Surface: Singletrack trail
Season: May through October
Fun factor: Views, incredible views, and more views

Getting there: From Main Street in Ketchum, drive north. Turn left at the streetlight onto Warm Springs Road. Follow this road as it winds through a Ketchum business district, past the skate park, and over the Big Wood River. Approximately 2 miles from Ketchum, at the four-way stop sign, turn left leading to the base of the Warm Springs side of Bald Mountain. The trailhead is located at the base of the ski run, next to the lodge, on the slope-side of the ski run, across the bridge over troubled waters (Warm Springs).

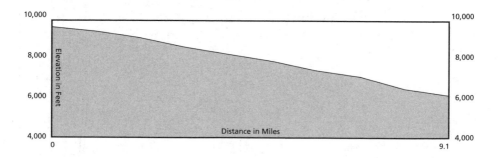

25b Cold Springs Trail

If you're riding up this side of the mountain, it is rather steep until you reach the Cold Springs chairlift. From here, it's gradual cruising up and around the south side of the mountain, eventually reaching the top. If you're riding down, be cautious of other riders and hikers moving in your opposite direction.

Distance: 8.6 miles
Difficulty rating: Moderate
Technical rating: 2
The ride: One-way
Starting elevation: 9,010 feet
Ending elevation: 5,680 feet

Total elevation gain/loss: 3,330 feet
Surface: Singletrack trail
Season: May through October
Fun factor: Views, incredible views, and more views

Getting there: From the Main Street (Highway 75) and Sun Valley Road stoplight in Ketchum, go west on Third Street heading toward the mountain. After 4 blocks, the road takes a natural left and becomes Third Avenue. Follow this road as it winds its way to the River Run base area and parking lot. Park here and backtrack on your bike about 100 feet to the bike path and ride south approximately 2 miles. Turn right at the trailhead sign and begin riding up Cold Springs Canyon. If you passed under the highway on the bike path, you've gone about 100 yards too far.

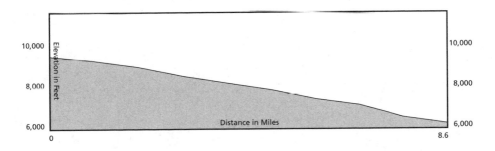

25c Lower River Run Trail

This is a great post-work, quick ride that'll get you from one side of Bald Mountain to the other. It also provides great access to the top of the mountain. There are maps the entire way, so you'll have to seriously try hard to get lost.

Distance: 9 miles
Difficulty rating: Moderate
Technical rating: 1+
The ride: One-way
Starting elevation: 5,680 feet
High point elevation: 7,350 feet

Total elevation gain: 1,670 feet
Surface: Singletrack trail
Season: May through October
Fun factor: Views, incredible views, and more views

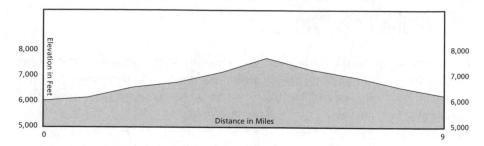

Getting there: From the Main Street (Highway 75) and Sun Valley Road stoplight in Ketchum, go west on Third Street heading toward the mountain. After 4 blocks, the road takes a natural left and becomes Third Avenue. Follow this road as it winds its way to the River Run base area of the mountain. Park anywhere near the base area in the parking lots. Mount up and ride over the bridge between the two large buildings and veer right of the ski lift and look for the trailhead taking off left under the lift. It is 5 miles of casual climbing before the descent into Warm Springs. From there, take the roads back into town and back to the River Run side of Bald Mountain and your car.

Ride connectors: You can link and link and link multiple rides in this area, as well as into Fox Creek, Chocolate Gulch, and farther north—all on singletrack. This whole part of Ketchum singletrack is what made this place a mountain biking mecca!

26 Adams Gulch Area Rides

Adams Gulch is a heavily used area due to its close proximity to Ketchum. The trails here are used by hikers, trail runners, mountain bikers, and equestrians. Please be considerate of others using the trails and stay in complete control while descending. Ride mileages may vary depending on where you start. Some mileages are listed as "one-way," which doesn't mean it is rideable only in one direction, but rather the mileage is only from one end of the ride to the other.

Getting there: From Ketchum, drive north on Highway 75 for 1.5 miles and turn left at the sign for ADAMS GULCH ROAD. Follow this road down and through the subdivision, crossing over the river and veering right. You drive in from the highway through a subdivision and the road comes to a T-intersection. You turn left there and continue immediately through a ranch-style gate (log gateway). There are also USFS signs to direct users to the correct place, so there is very little chance of getting lost. You gain the trailhead and parking area about 0.5 mile later. All rides begin here.

An open area is often the calm before the storm.

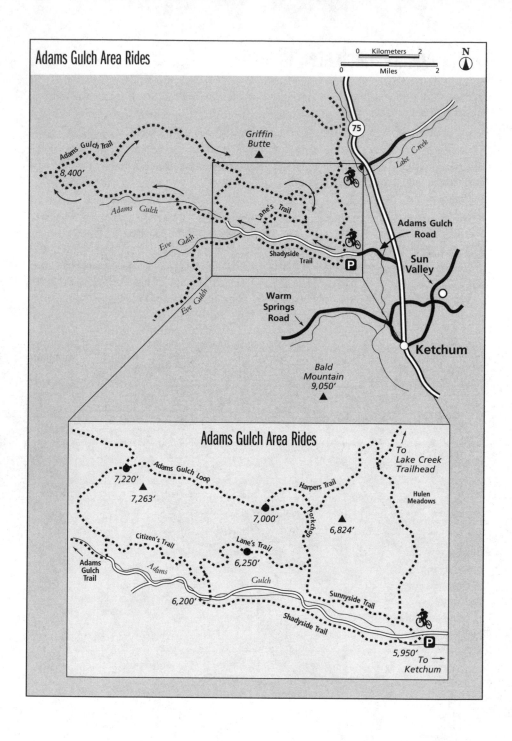

Adams Gulch Area Rides

0 Kilometers 2
0 Miles 2

N

Griffin Butte ▲

Lake Creek

75

Adams Gulch Trail 8,400'

Adams Gulch

Lane's Trail

Eve Gulch

Shadyside Trail

Eve Gulch

Adams Gulch Road

Sun Valley

P

Warm Springs Road

Ketchum

Bald Mountain 9,050' ▲

Adams Gulch Area Rides

To Lake Creek Trailhead

7,220' ●
7,263' ▲

Adams Gulch Loop

Harpers Trail

Hulen Meadows

7,000' ●

6,824' ▲

Citizen's Trail

Porkchop

Lane's Trail

Adams Gulch Trail

Adams

6,250' ●

Gulch

Sunnyside Trail

6,200'

Shadyside Trail

P

5,950'
To Ketchum

26a Adams Gulch Loop

Typically a clockwise ride, you get a great warm-up on the jeep road before hitting the singletrack, which is a constant grind to the top with periodic rests. Once topped out, the downhill is nothing short of spectacular. Well worth the work!

Distance: 7 miles
Difficulty rating: Difficult
Technical rating: 2+
The ride: Loop
Starting elevation: 5,950 feet
High point elevation: 7,220 feet

Total elevation gain: 1,270 feet
Surface: Dirt jeep road and singletrack trail
Season: Late May through October
Fun factor: The ultimate loop complete with the complimentary grind

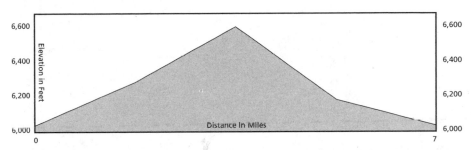

26b Lane's/Sunnyside Trails

While Shadyside is obviously in the shade, this one is directly opposite. You want sun? Come and get it! We like riding this one clockwise, due to the gradual warm-up on the jeep road. Once it hits the singletrack, you grind for a bit before backing off and topping out at a picnic table. From here, the descent is fun, fast, and furious.

Distance: 3.5 miles
Difficulty rating: Easy/Moderate
Technical rating: 1+
The ride: Loop
Starting elevation: 5,950 feet
High point elevation: 6,520 feet

Total elevation gain: 570 feet
Surface: Dirt jeep road and singletrack trail
Season: May through October
Fun factor: Picnic table rest at the top with phenomenal views

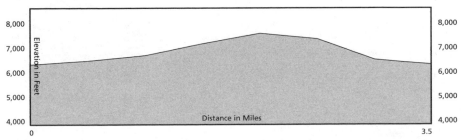

26c Shadyside Trail

This ride is never too technical or hard, aside from the start, which is not an indicator for the rest of the ride.

Distance: 3 miles
Difficulty rating: Easy/Moderate
Technical rating: 1+
The ride: Loop
Starting elevation: 5,950 feet
High point elevation: 6,200 feet

Total elevation gain: 250 feet
Surface: Dirt jeep road and singletrack trail
Season: Late May through October
Fun factor: Definite fun warm-up on a hot summer day

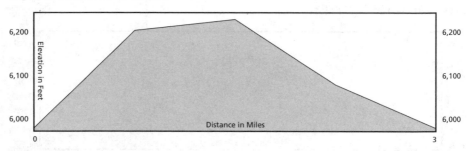

26d Adams Gulch Trail

This is a serious ride. It seems longer than it is due to its technical nature. Have the right attitude from the onset or don't go.

Distance: 14 miles
Difficulty rating: Abusive
Technical rating: 4
The ride: Loop
Starting elevation: 5,950 feet
High point elevation: 8,400 feet

Total elevation gain: 2,450 feet
Surface: Dirt jeep road and singletrack trail
Season: Late May through October
Fun factor: Defines the word fun—hills, views, and downhills

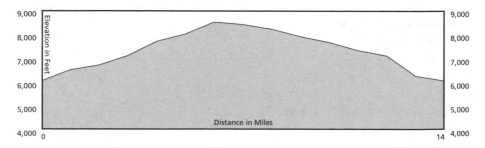

26e Harpers Trail

Great in either direction, but we personally like this one counterclockwise. A short grind leads to rollers into the Lake Creek area before gradual grinding up to the top where you encounter the Adams Gulch Loop descent.

Distance: 3.5 miles
Difficulty rating: Moderate
Technical rating: 2
The ride: Loop
Starting elevation: 5,950 feet
High point elevation: 7,000 feet

Total elevation gain: 1,050 feet
Surface: Singletrack trail
Season: Late May through October
Fun factor: Another great loop, which connects Fox Creek and Lake Creek into the Adams Gulch Area.

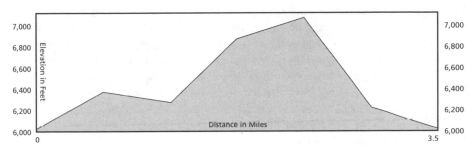

26f Citizen's Trail

This is a great cruiser in either direction, but if you want a bit more downhilling fun, ride it from Adams Gulch Loop into Lane's Trail.

Distance: 2+ miles
Difficulty rating: Easy/Moderate
Technical rating: 1
The ride: Loop
Starting elevation: 6,400 feet
High point elevation: 6,550 feet
Total elevation gain: 310 feet

Surface: Singletrack trail
Season: Late May through October
Fun factor: This is the newest trail in the Adams Gulch Area, completed in spring 2005 and built by the locals with oversight by the USFS. It is a great connector trail between Lane's and Adams Gulch Loop.

27 Fox Creek

This is undoubtedly one of the best all-around rides close to Ketchum. Never too steep to ride and always a good time on the downhills.

Distance: 6.6 miles
Difficulty rating: Moderate
Technical rating: 1+
The ride: Loop
Starting elevation: 5,950 feet
High point elevation: 6,700 feet

Total elevation gain: 750 feet
Surface: Singletrack trail and dirt jeep road
Season: Late May through October
Fun factor: Moderate climbs, great descents, and wildflowers

Getting there: From Ketchum, drive north on Highway 75 for 4 miles to the Lake Creek trailhead and turn left into the parking lot. The ride begins here. (**Note:** Access to the Lake Creek trailhead may be hindered by flood waters in early season. If this is the case, turn around and drive back 0.5 mile on the highway to Hulen Meadows Road and turn right. Follow the road across the bridge, and park on the right immediately in the gravel parking area. Ride up the road staying right until the cul-de-sac. Follow the trail next to the driveway heading north at the end of the cul-de-sac. In 0.25 mile, you join up with the main Lake Creek Trail coming in from the right.) (**FYI:** There is also a trailhead for this ride located approximately 7 miles north of Ketchum on the west side of the highway.)

Miles and Directions

0.0 From the Lake Creek trailhead parking lot, ride across the steel bridge and the Big Wood River. Follow this trail as it winds to the right through the trees and next to the river.

0.2 Ride up a small embankment to where it intersects with a jeep road. Turn right here.

0.6 Trail junction. The left fork here is where the Fox Creek Loop comes out. Stay straight on the jeep trail heading north.

1.3 The jeep road turns to singletrack and quickly comes to a shale/rock traverse. After roller-coastering along, you will cross two small bridges.

1.9 An intensely steep switchback leads up and away from the river, followed by a similarly steep downhill and a quick slalom course through the aspen trees.

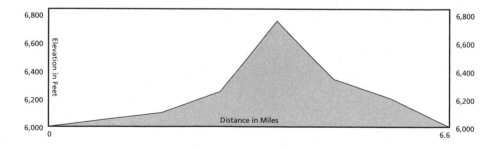

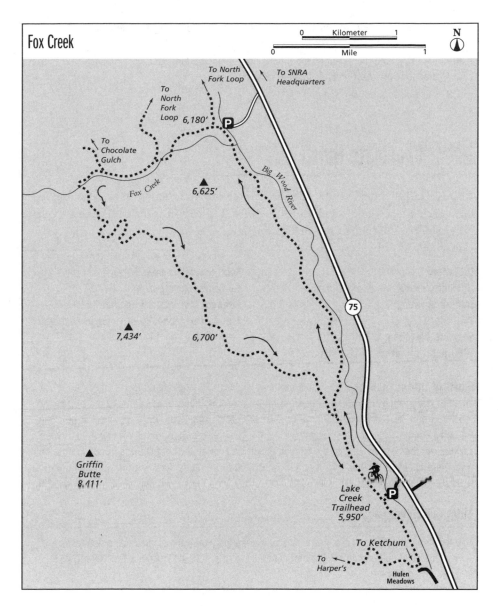

Fox Creek

0   Kilometer   1

0   Mile   1

N

To North
Fork Loop

To SNRA
Headquarters

To
North
Fork
Loop   6,180'

P

To
Chocolate
Gulch

Fox Creek

6,625'

Big Wood River

7,434'

6,700'

75

Griffin
Butte
8,111'

Lake
Creek
Trailhead
5,950'

P

To Ketchum

To
Harper's

Hulen
Meadows

2.4   Cross over Fox Creek and come to a trail junction. Turn left here on Fox Creek Trail. The right fork will put you on the North Fork Trail.

2.6   Another trail junction. Take the left (straight) fork to continue heading upstream into Fox Creek. The right fork leads into the upper section of the North Fork Loop.

3.1   After crossing over two bridges, you reach another trail junction. Stay on the left (straight) fork heading upstream into Fox Creek. The right fork leads to Oregon Gulch and/or Chocolate Gulch. From here, the trail becomes a one-way-only trail for mountain bikers. Be cautious here, runners and hikers could be coming in the other direction. After a couple 100 yards, cross over Fox Creek and begin a gradual climb up switchbacks.

4.1 Come to a saddle and continue on. The faint trail off to the right of the trail here leads to a nice bench in the meadow.

6.0 Join the main trail again as the loop is now complete. Turn right and continue back to the trailhead at Lake Creek or Hulen Meadows.

6.6 Back at your car and the end of the ride.

28 Chocolate Gulch

This is a rather short but fun ride that has moderate climbing, creek crossings, technical rock moves, views, and a great descent. On top of that, it has access to three other rides in the immediate surrounding area.

Distance: 3.8 miles
Difficulty rating: Moderate/Difficult
Technical rating: 2+
The ride: Loop
Starting elevation: 6,150 feet
High point elevation: 6,750 feet

Total elevation gain: 600 feet
Surface: Singletrack trail
Season: Mid-May through late October
Fun factor: Moderate climbing to incredible views of the Wood River Valley

Getting there: From Ketchum, drive north on Highway 75 approximately 6.8 miles and turn left on Chocolate Gulch Road (just after crossing over the Big Wood River). Drive to the end of the road and park here. This parking area can usually get crowded so please respect the private property and only park in the designated area. If it is too crowded in the parking area, please choose another ride or park at the Oregon Gulch parking area about 0.5 mile north on the highway. There is also a trailhead for this ride located approximately 7 miles north of Ketchum on the west side of the highway.

Miles and Directions

0.0 From the parking area, ride west and immediately onto the singletrack, which takes a quick switchback to the left and gradually climbs a bit to Chocolate Gulch Trail 149B. Turn right here.

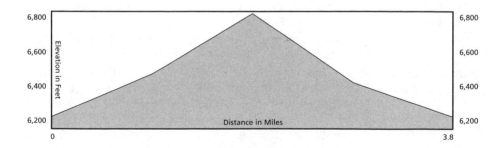

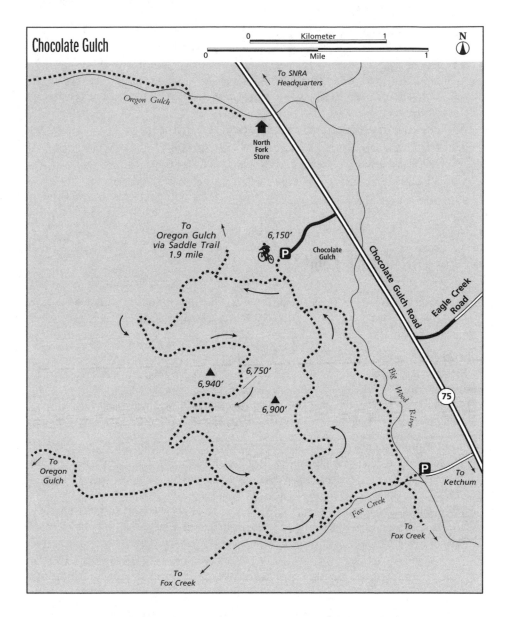

Chocolate Gulch

0   Kilometer   1

0   Mile   1

N

Oregon Gulch

To SNRA
Headquarters

North
Fork
Store

To
Oregon Gulch
via Saddle Trail
1.9 mile

6,150'

Chocolate
Gulch

Chocolate Gulch Road

Eagle Creek
Road

6,750'

▲
6,940'

▲
6,900'

Big Wood River

75

To
Oregon
Gulch

P

To
Ketchum

Fox Creek

To
Fox Creek

To
Fox Creek

0.3   After crossing a small bridge, a muddy bog, and the stream, take a sharp left around the willows and start a gradual climb, passing by the right fork for Saddle Trail, which leads over the hills to Oregon Gulch (1.9 miles long).

0.6   Forge another stream crossing, leading to moderate climbing.

1.5   Top of the first saddle. This is a false summit; keep going, almost there!

1.7   Top of the second saddle and the high point of the ride. Continue on down the trail passing by a difficult rock/sand/scree pile and into a couple of switchbacks. Be careful here, the trail could be fairly loose.

2.1 Trail junction. The left fork is the continuation of the Chocolate Gulch trail, while the right fork is the Oregon Gulch/Fox Creek Loop 149C. Make a left turn here.

2.4 Trail junction. The left fork is the continuation of Chocolate Gulch Trail along with Fox Creek Loop (you are now on one trail with two different names). Don't get confused; just look at the sign. Go left here. Taking the right trail would lead to the upper section of Fox Creek.

2.7 After a few roller-coasters, you cross over Fox Creek on two bridges.

2.9 Trail junction. Take the left fork here on North Fork Loop 149A and start climbing up a switchback. It seems steep but is relatively short.

3.5 Junction with the lower section of the North Fork Loop. Continue straight.

3.8 Back at the trailhead and the end of the ride.

29 North Fork Loop

The North Fork Loop is usually considered as a starting point for other rides. However, the loop in itself is a great warm-up for Chocolate Gulch or Fox Creek.

Distance: 2.6 miles
Difficulty rating: Moderate
Technical rating: 2+
The ride: Loop
Starting elevation: 6,150 feet

High point elevation: 6,350 feet
Total elevation gain: 200 feet
Surface: Singletrack trail
Season: Early May through late October
Fun factor: Quick, technical, views, and river

Getting there: From Ketchum, drive north on Highway 75 approximately 6.8 miles and turn left on Chocolate Gulch Road (just after crossing over the Big Wood River). Drive to the end of the road and park here. This parking area can usually get a bit crowded so please respect the private property and only park in the designated area. If it is too crowded in the parking area, please choose another ride or park in the Oregon Gulch parking area about 0.5 mile north on the highway. There is also a trailhead for this ride located approximately 7 miles north of Ketchum on the west side of the highway.

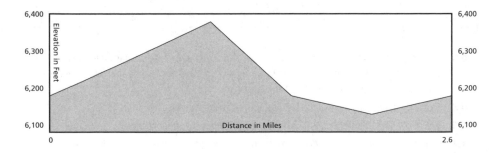

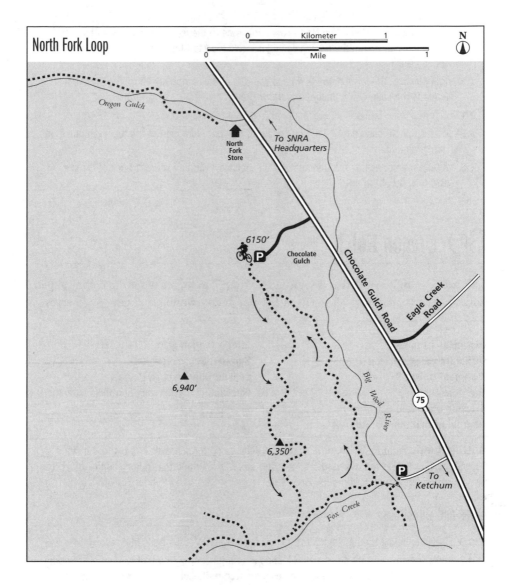

Miles and Directions

0.0 From the parking area, ride west and immediately onto the singletrack, which takes a quick switchback to the left and gradually climbs a bit passing Chocolate Gulch Trail 149B on the right. Stay straight on the main trail here.

0.3 Junction with North Fork Loop Trail 149A. Go right here. From here, be careful as the trail crosses over a steep hillside and rocks.

0.4 Gain a small saddle then immediately drop into a creek and immediately a short hill.

1.0 After the trail roller-coasters a bit, you gain another saddle and begin the descent into Fox Creek.

1.3 Junction with Fox Creek. The North Fork Loop goes to the left here. If you want to combine any other ride in the area, going right would lead to Chocolate Gulch, Fox Creek, or Oregon Gulch.

1.5 Trail junction. The left fork leads on into the rest of the North Fork Loop. The right fork leads to the Lake Creek trailhead and Fox Creek.

2.1 Skinny bridge; be careful here, especially when it is wet.

2.3 A steep pitch leads back to the beginning of the loop. Turn right at the top, continuing on the same trail.

2.6 After passing back by the Chocolate Gulch trailhead you find yourself back at the car and the end of the ride.

30 Oregon Gulch

This is one of those rides that is such a great time, you forget about the technical part instantly. Rock outcrops will test your balance and downhills will test your nerves.

Distance: 11 miles
Difficulty rating: Difficult
Technical rating: 2+
The ride: Loop
Starting elevation: 6,250 feet
High point elevation: 7,600 feet

Total elevation gain: 2,310 feet
Surface: Singletrack trail
Season: June through October
Fun factor: Climbs, long downhills, streams, wildflowers

Getting there: From Ketchum, drive north on Highway 75 for just over 7 miles to the North Fork Store. Turn left on the dirt road just past the store and behind the trailers. Follow this back to a grassy meadow with bathrooms. Park here.

Miles and Directions

0.0 Begin by riding up the singletrack trail on the west side of the parking area.

0.2 After entering into the trees, you will encounter a junction with a trail leading over Saddle Trail (1.9 miles long) on the left and eventually into Chocolate Gulch. Instead, stay straight on the main trail, which quickly goes down and over the creek where the trail continues up the gulch on the north side of the creek. This is Oregon Gulch.

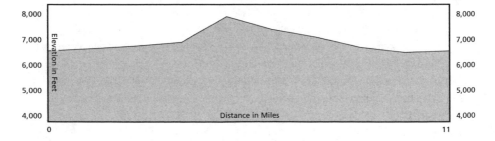

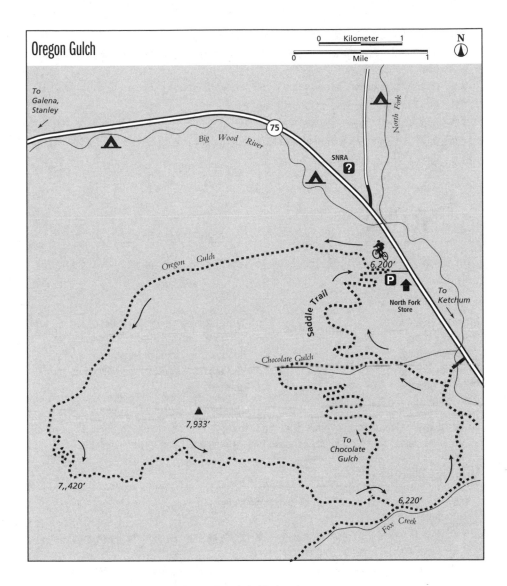

Oregon Gulch

To Galena, Stanley

Big Wood River

75

North Fork

SNRA ?

6,200'

Oregon Gulch

Saddle Trail

P

North Fork Store

To Ketchum

Chocolate Gulch

7,933'

To Chocolate Gulch

7,,420'

6,220'

Fox Creek

1.3 Cross through the gate (please close it behind you).

3.2 Trail junction. Turn left here and cross the creek heading toward Fox Creek. The right fork goes up and eventually into the East Fork of Baker Creek.

4.6 Saddle, watch for the sharp right turn in about 100 yards.

5.0 Climb to a saddle and turn left into the gulch. The more worn right fork just climbs to a small overlook. From here, the trail becomes a technical steep downhill with loose dirt and rocks.

7.0 Trail junction. Turn right and continue on Oregon/Fox Creek Loop 149C. The left fork climbs up and over into Chocolate Gulch on Trail 146B.

7.25 Trail junction. Turn left and head downstream with Fox Creek.

7.5 After a few roller-coasters, you cross over Fox Creek on two bridges.

7.7 Trail junction. Take the left fork here on the North Fork Loop 149A and start up a switch-back to a saddle.

8.3 Pass by the junction with the lower section of the North Fork Loop.

8.6 Turn left at the sign leading to Chocolate Gulch.

8.9 Turn right at the sign leading to Saddle Trail.

10.8 Back at the junction with Oregon Gulch Trail. Turn right here.

11.0 Back at your car and the end of the ride.

31 Fox Peak

This is not a first–date ride. Be ready for going over the front of your bike, falling, and pushing.

Distance: 22.4 miles
Difficulty rating: Abusive
Technical rating: 4
The ride: One-way
Starting elevation: 6,675 feet
High point elevation: 8,720 feet

Total elevation gain: 2,045 feet
Surface: Dirt jeep road to singletrack trail
Season: June through October
Fun factor: Wicked downhills, climbs, and traverses

Getting there: From Ketchum, drive north on Highway 75 approximately 15.5 miles and park on the right side of the road directly opposite Baker Creek Road. The ride begins here.

Miles and Directions

0.0 From the parking area, cross back over the highway and begin riding up Baker Creek Road 162.

3.1 Just after crossing over the East Fork of Baker Creek, turn left onto the East Fork of Baker Creek Road 68 and begin a gradual climb.

5.1 At the fork, take the lower (left), more traveled road, which descends for a bit before climbing again.

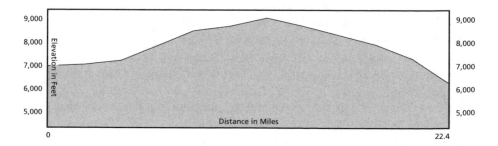

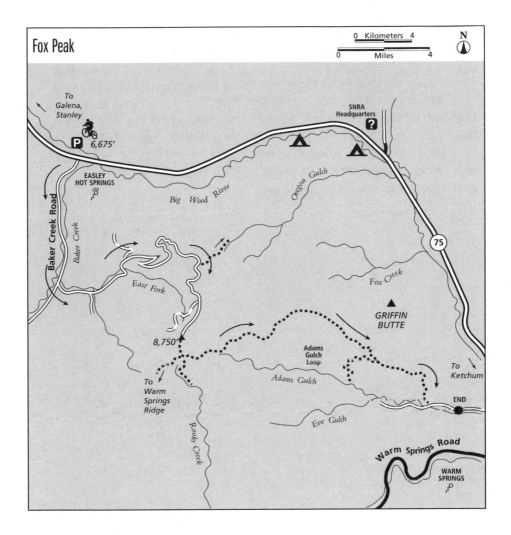

Fox Peak

0 Kilometers 4

0 Miles 4

N

To Galena, Stanley

P 6,675'

SNRA Headquarters
?

EASLEY HOT SPRINGS

Oregon Gulch

Big Wood River

Baker Creek Road

Baker Creek

East Fork

Fox Creek

75

8,750'

GRIFFIN BUTTE

To Warm Springs Ridge

Adams Gulch Loop

Adams Gulch

To Ketchum

Rooks Creek

Eve Gulch

END

Warm Springs Road

WARM SPRINGS

5.7 When you come to the next fork, take the upper (right), more traveled road and begin climbing another pitch.

6.3 Encounter the switchbacks, which are never too hard.

8.0 The saddle with a view. Continue on the jeep road passing by the trailhead to the Easley Loop around the next corner.

9.6 Pass by the Oregon Gulch trailhead on the left.

9.7 Begin a fast descent on the jeep road, but keep a watch for a singletrack turn-off in another 1.6 miles. It's easy to miss, unless you mean to.

11.3 Sign on the left says trail for Fox Creek and Adams Gulch. You can go this way if you want, but you'll have to push a bit. Instead, stay on the main road.

12.3 At the major intersection, stay left!

12.6 The double track dead ends at a berm. Singletrack starts on the back side.

13.0 Trail junction. Stay left on Trail 142 to Adams Gulch.

14.0 Gain a small grassy saddle and begin a quick, exciting downhill.

14.2 Trail junction. The right fork leads into the top of Adams Gulch. Instead, stay straight on the main trail traversing the hillside. From here to the junction with Adams Gulch Loop, the trail is rocky, loose, and intense in some places.

17.8 After climbing a short steep hill, the trail traverses down and into Adams Gulch.

19.3 Trail junction. You are now at the top of the Adams Gulch Loop Trail. Either direction (left or right) will take you down to the trailhead. But why not keep the fun rolling? Turn left.

20.2 Harpers Trail takes off to the left, but stay straight on Adams Gulch Loop.

22.4 The end of the ride and the parking area.

Riding in the Copper Basin Area

When you think of Copper Basin, thoughts of dusty roads and mining tailings come to mind. Think again. We've only highlighted two rides in the area, one of which is currently closed, but there are a plethora of opportunities over there. Don't be afraid to be adventurous. The two open rides in this area, just happen to be two of our favorites, so take that for what it's worth.

While driving to this area, many cars have gotten flats from the sharp rocks on the roads. However, we have seen even the lowest sportscars driving on the roads. For an extra adventure after riding in the area, drive up and over Antelope Pass, which will take you towards Arco and Mackay. Enjoy some eats at Grandpa's BBQ in Arco, world famous!

Be adventurous and have some serious fun . . . go to Copper Basin!

Biking is a great family adventure.

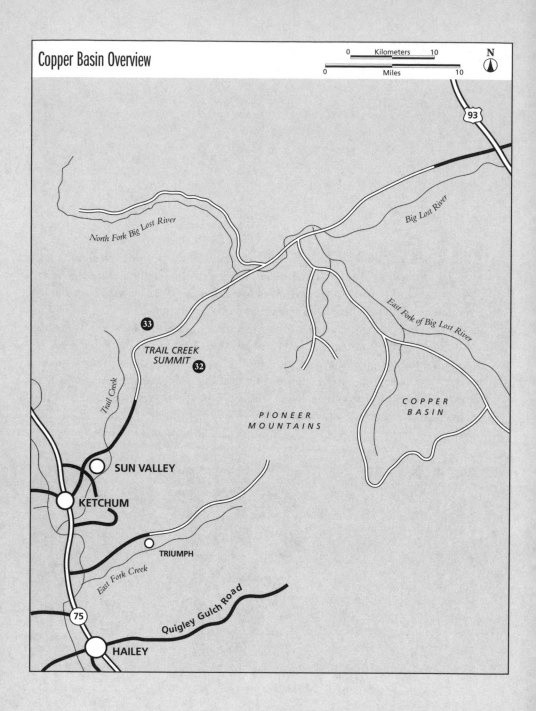

Copper Basin Overview

Kilometers
0   10
0   10
Miles

N

93

North Fork Big Lost River

Big Lost River

East Fork of Big Lost River

33

TRAIL CREEK
SUMMIT   32

Trail Creek

COPPER
BASIN

PIONEER
MOUNTAINS

SUN VALLEY

KETCHUM

TRIUMPH

East Fork Creek

Quigley Gulch Road

75

HAILEY

32 Park Creek

Park Creek is one of those hidden wonders in the Copper Basin area, where beautiful canyons, creeks, fishing, and camping make for an entire weekend experience. The trail is a bit rough in places, but has recently been redone to make it a soon-to-be-classic.

Distance: 12.4 miles
Difficulty rating: Moderate
Technical rating: 2+
The ride: Out-and-back
Starting elevation: 7,646 feet
High point elevation: 8,500 feet

Total elevation gain: 854 feet
Surface: Dirt jeep road and singletrack trail
Season: Late May through October
Fun factor: Gorgeous canyon, wildlife, and trail-finding

Getting there: From the Main Street/Sun Valley Road intersection in Ketchum, drive east toward Sun Valley, passing the resort complex area, and continue on up the road, which eventually becomes Trail Creek Road. After 12.5 miles, you reach Trail Creek Summit. Continue on the main road for another 0.7 mile and park on the left at the junction of Park Creek Road 140 and Trail Creek Road. The ride begins here.

Miles and Directions

0.0 Begin by riding up Road 140 heading north and west through a large meadow.

1.2 Road to the left leads to High Ridge Trail trailhead. Continue on Park Creek Road up the canyon. For the next 1.5 miles, you'll encounter many primitive campsites and meadows.

2.6 Road ends and singletrack continues on.

2.7 Major stream crossing over Park Creek.

3.9 Whoa! Look for the cairn on the right of the road to show you where to cross the creek (A little ways farther, the main road fades away into nothing). Instead, cross the creek, look for a faint trail leading uphill and into some trees. There you'll find a better trail leading left (north). This is not too difficult to find. Sounds difficult, but it's not.

4.3 A stream crossing leads to a series of springs and mud bogs.

4.7 Encounter another small meadow with bogs.

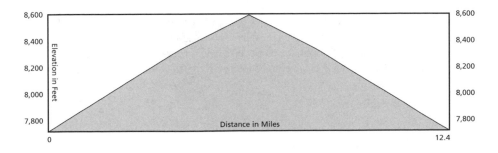

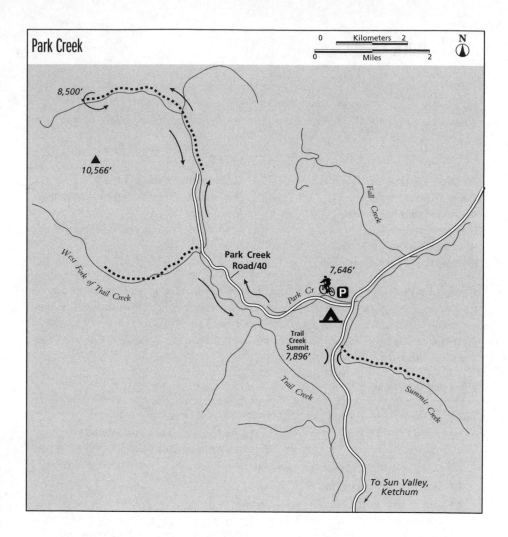

Park Creek

0 Kilometers 2

0 Miles 2

N

8,500'

10,566'

West Fork of Trail Creek

Park Creek
Road/40

Park Cr

7,646'

Fall Creek

Trail
Creek
Summit
7,896'

Trail Creek

Summit Creek

To Sun Valley,
Ketchum

4.9   Whoa! After a steep crossing over a small creek, veer left on the other side of the creek following the contour of the creek and looking for the cairns.

5.0   Be sure to follow the trail heading left at all of the downed timber. From here, the trail begins climbing up the canyon following the creek at all times.

5.4   The trail contours the creek at a very steep angle here.

6.2   The end of the ride is at the edge of the completely downed forest in front of you. After exploring farther up the canyon from here, I'm convinced that a chainsaw is mandatory equipment; I just haven't found the proper bike mount . . . yet. Turn around and retrace your route. This ride could be an even better loop if someone had the will and power to do some logging.

12.4 Back at your car and the end of the ride.

33 Lake Creek (Copper Basin)

Truly one of the classics of Copper Basin. Put your fun-hat on and get ready for a great ride amidst lakes and the Pioneer Mountains.

Distance: 13.8 miles
Difficulty rating: Difficult
Technical rating: 2+
The ride: Loop
Starting elevation: 8,080 feet
High point elevation: 9,650 feet

Total elevation gain: 1,570 feet
Surface: Singletrack trail
Season: June through October
Fun factor: The Pioneer Mountains, lakes, and great fishing

Getting there: From the Main Street/Sun Valley Road intersection in Ketchum drive east toward Sun Valley passing the resort complex, and continue up the road, which eventually becomes Trail Creek Road. After reaching the summit at 12.5 miles, you reach Trail Creek Summit. Drive 10.3 miles to Wildhorse/Copper Basin Road 135. Turn right and drive down the road 2 miles to the junction of Copper Basin Road and Wildhorse Creek Road. Turn left here and drive another 16 dusty miles (it's worth it), turning right at the second Copper Basin Loop Road sign. Cruise another 4.5 miles up the road to the Lake Creek turn-off. Park; the ride begins here.

Miles and Directions

0.0 Begin by riding up the trail, slowly winding your way up the valley, eventually getting to a rather large meadow.

3.9 At the fork near the cabin, turn left and get ready for a bit of a grind.

6.1 Catch your breath and pass by the trail over to Round Lake, the first of four lakes.

6.6 Cruise past Long Lake, or stop to cool off.

7.5 After a short steep pitch, you arrive at Rough Lake.

8.6 The final of four lakes, Big Lake, is reached after a short, gradual ascent.

9.8 Back at the original start of the lollipop loop. Turn left and continue back to the trailhead.

13.8 End of the ride and back at your car.

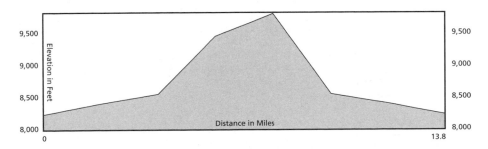

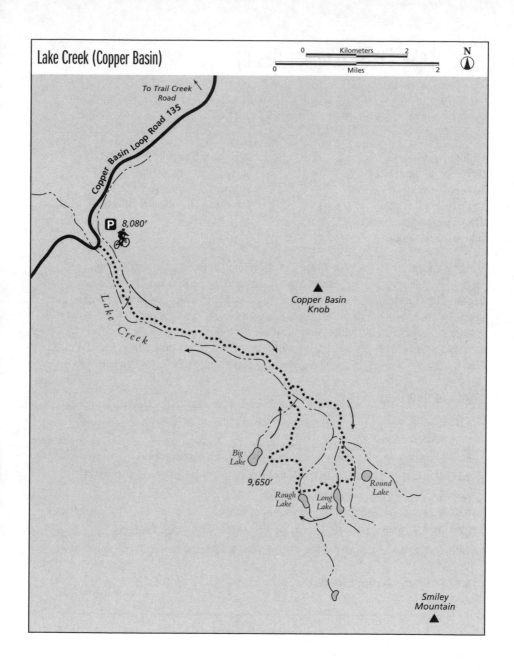

Kilometers

Miles

N

To Trail Creek
Road

Copper Basin Loop Road 135

Lake Creek

P 8,080'

Copper Basin
Knob

Big
Lake

9,650'

Rough
Lake

Long
Lake

Round
Lake

Smiley
Mountain

Riding in the North Valley and Galena Area

When you choose to ride in the Galena Area, you will be blessed with amazing scenery, wildlife, incredible trails, and not many people close to you. One of the riding gems in this area is Galena Lodge. Between the trails, food, staff, views, and ambience, you WILL be blown away. There are some new trails around the area, and what a perfect staging area—a south-facing deck in the mountains!

The Harriman Trail ends or begins at Galena Lodge. It's a rolling gravel and dirt trail that parallels the highway back in the trees. Great location for a family cruise or hardcores wanting to get their butts worked.

Other North Valley rides, such as Easley Hot Springs Loop/Curly's and Prairie Lake to Miner Lake Loop will certainly work parts of your body other than your legs. Can you say mental strength?! For a real adventure that's no exaggeration, get on the Baker Lake to Norton Creek ride. You will be amazed at the views, trail-finding skills you'll need, and incredible, faint trails! Be prepared for anything if you go there.

Galena Overview

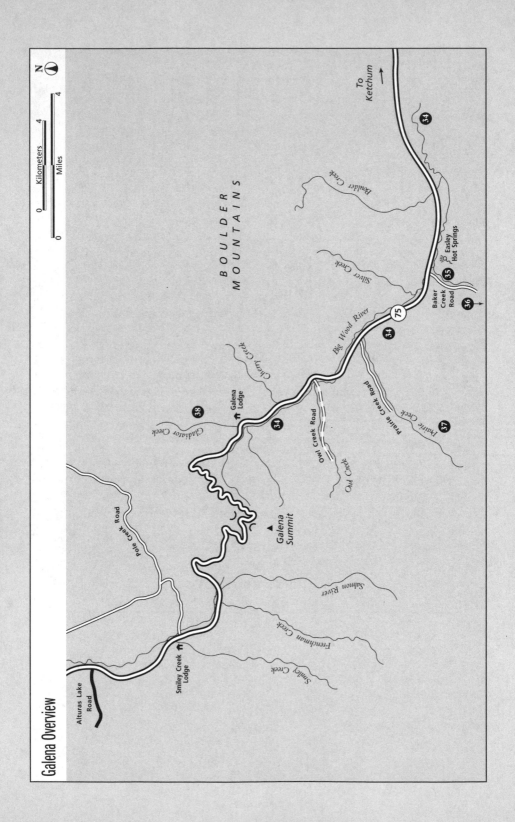

34 Harriman Trail

The Harriman Trail extends from the SNRA headquarters north of Ketchum all the way up to Galena Lodge. You can either ride up or down the trail, but don't be fooled into thinking it's gradual the entire way. This trail definitely has some ups and downs and is the perfect ride for a cyclocross bike. This ride is the perfect introductory ride for the person new to mountain biking or visiting the valley. Because of its beautifully manicured terrain, you can enjoy this ride and still maintain a conversation. This could be classified as the perfect first-date ride. No pressure to perform, no tears, good conversation . . .

Distance: 18.6 miles (one-way)
Difficulty rating: Easy/Moderate
Technical rating: 1+
The ride: Start anywhere along the trail and enjoy!
Starting elevation: 7,290 feet
Ending elevation: 6,280 feet

Total elevation loss: 1,010 feet
Surface: 12-foot wide pea-gravel trail
Season: May through October
Fun factor: Beautiful cruise up or down the valley following the Big Wood River and the Boulder Mountains all the way

Getting there: From Ketchum, drive north on Highway 75 for 7.8 miles. Turn right into the parking area for the Sawtooth National Recreation Area headquarters. This is the end point of the ride. For a shuttle, leave a car here and continue driving up Highway 75 for another 16.2 miles (24 miles total). Turn right into the Galena Lodge parking lot. Follow the signs, the ride begins here. Of course, you can always start anywhere along the trail and go anywhere.

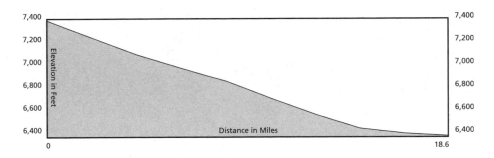

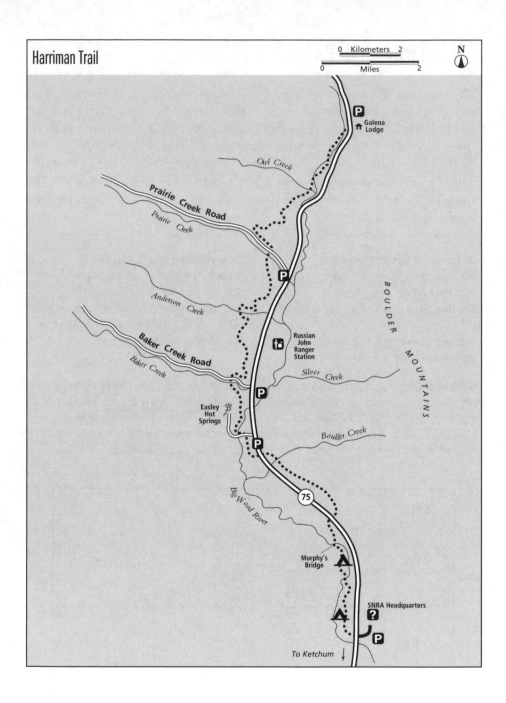

Harriman Trail

N

0　Kilometers　2

0　Miles　2

Galena Lodge

Owl Creek

Prairie Creek Road

Prairie Creek

Anderson Creek

Baker Creek Road

Baker Creek

Russian John Ranger Station

Silver Creek

Easley Hot Springs

Boulder Creek

BOULDER MOUNTAINS

Big Wood River

75

Murphy's Bridge

SNRA Headquarters

To Ketchum

35 Easley Hot Springs Loop (Curly's)

A gradual climb on a jeep road to a singletrack downhill that rivals any ride in the area.

Distance: 12.3 miles
Difficulty rating: Moderate
Technical rating: 3 (for the descent)
The ride: Loop
Starting elevation: 6,675 feet
High point elevation: 8,200 feet

Total elevation gain: 1,525 feet
Surface: Dirt jeep road and singletrack trail
Season: June through October
Fun factor: Steady moderate climb to an outrageous downhill

Getting there: From Ketchum, drive north on Highway 75 approximately 15.5 miles and park on the right side of the road directly opposite Baker Creek Road. The ride begins here.

Miles and Directions

0.0 From the parking area, cross back over the highway and begin riding up Baker Creek Road 162.

3.1 Just after crossing over the East Fork of Baker Creek, turn left onto the East Fork of Baker Creek Road 68 and begin a gradual climb.

5.1 At the fork, take the lower (left), more traveled road, which descends for a bit before climbing again.

5.7 Another fork. Take the right (upper), more traveled road and begin climbing another pitch.

6.3 Switchbacks: never too hard, but always a good get.

8.0 The saddle with a view and the top of the ride. Although the jeep road keeps going past this point, the top is marked by the end of the switchback and a small turn-out on the left of the road next to a small tree. Great views to the west.

8.2 Whoa! While making a right turn on the road, look for the faint jeep trail leading off to the left, which quickly becomes a great singletrack descent heading down the ridgeline.

8.6 Pass by a watering hole and views of the Boulder Mountains.

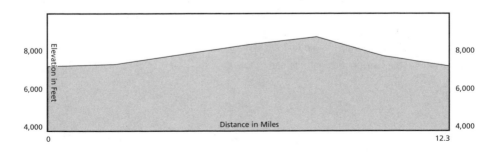

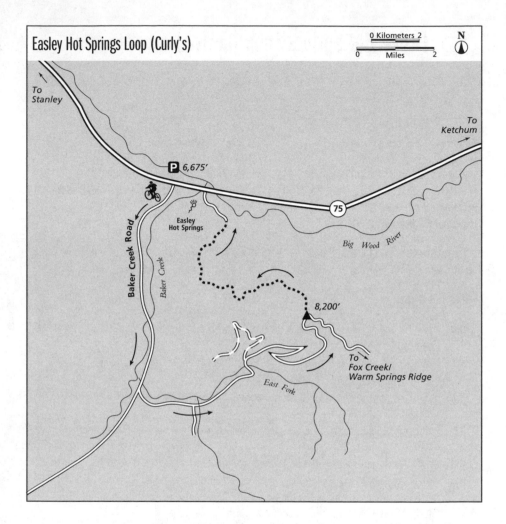

Easley Hot Springs Loop (Curly's)

0 Kilometers 2
0 Miles 2

N

To Stanley

To Ketchum

P 6,675'

Easley Hot Springs

75

Big Wood River

Baker Creek Road

Baker Creek

8,200'

To Fox Creek/ Warm Springs Ridge

East Fork

10.7 Begin a rather steep descent down the ridgeline. Please avoid skidding here (or going over the bars for that matter); it has become a big problem. If you can't descend without skidding, think about walking your bike through this section.

11.5 The trail comes out next to some cabins; please don't bother the people here. Continue on the dirt roads paralleling the highway until riding onto the highway a couple hundred yards later.

11.7 Turn left onto Highway 75 and ride back to your car.

12.3 Back at the parking area and the end of the ride.

You can almost hear it calling you. ▶

36 Baker Lake to Norton Creek

This is also known as Apollo Creek Trail. This is a faith ride. Believe and you're in; don't, and you might as well not leave your car. Enjoy!

Distance: 12.1 miles
Difficulty rating: Difficult
Technical rating: 3+
The ride: Loop
Starting elevation: 7,300 feet
High point elevation: 9,280 feet

Total elevation gain: 1,980 feet
Surface: Dirt jeep road and singletrack trail
Season: June through October
Fun factor: Fun? Definitely. Adventurous? You know it.

Getting there: From Ketchum, drive north on Highway 75 for 15.5 miles and turn left onto Baker Creek Road. Continue on another 6 miles to the junction with Norton and Prairie Lakes Roads and park on the right at the junction. The ride begins here. (**Note:** This trail may be closed to mountain bikes in the near future; please obey any signs indicating this.)

Miles and Directions

0.0 Begin by riding south on Baker Creek Road and up eventually to the Baker Lake parking lot at the end of the road.

3.4 The Baker Lake parking area. Ride across the creek, register yourself, and continue up the trail. The trail from here is not too steep . . .

4.9 Take the right fork leading off to Apollo Creek on Trail 139. From here you'll do a traversing descent before grinding and pushing a bit. Here's the faith part of the ride. Follow the cairns and red tape attached to the trees. Pay attention; it's easy to miss them.

5.2 The trail disappears into the meadow. Stay in the dry creek bed, watching for the cairns leading to a tree 150 yards later, where the trail reappears and switchbacks a bit before gaining a small saddle.

5.8 First saddle: Walk down the scree and begin riding at the edge of the rocks following cairns and red tape for almost a mile.

6.5 Reach the dry creek bed of Apollo Creek. Continue up the other side to the fork in the trail. As the sign indicates, straight ahead is Baker Lake Trail 138. The right fork leads down into Apollo Creek Trail 139. Stay straight traversing along Baker Lake Trail.

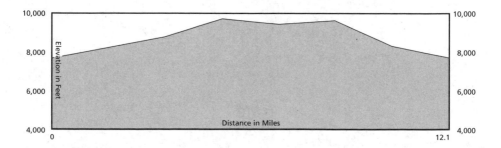

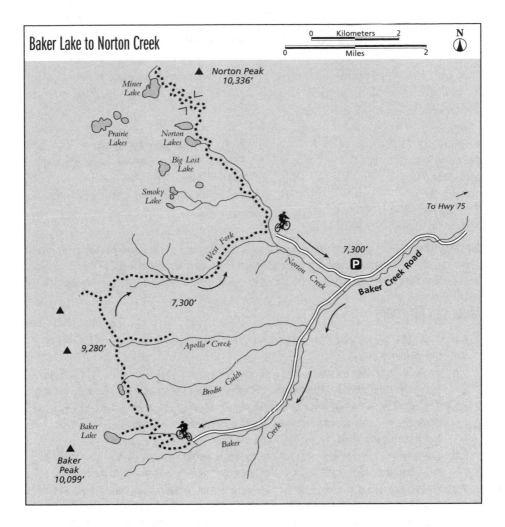

Baker Lake to Norton Creek

7.3 Gain the saddle leading into the West Fork of Norton Creek drainage. This is where all the fun begins, a great trail and descent.

7.6 Fork in the trail. Turn right into the West Fork of Norton Creek drainage. A left turn here would lead into Bluff and Big Smoky Creeks in the South Fork of the Boise River drainage.

10.7 Junction with Norton Creek, Norton Lakes Trail 135 and the trailhead parking area. Ride across the creek, through the parking area and continue on down the jeep road to your car.

12.1 End of the ride.

37 Prairie Lake to Miner Lake Loop

Not only is this a great nordic ski area, but the mountain biking here is phenomenal as well. Technical skills are helpful but not necessary; the grade is gradual and the scenery and swimming is even better!

Distance: 15.7 miles
Difficulty rating: Difficult
Technical rating: 4
The ride: Loop
Starting elevation: 6,900 feet
High point elevation: 8,700 feet

Total elevation gain: 1,800 feet
Surface: Dirt jeep road and singletrack trail
Season: June through October
Fun factor: Lakes, creeks, mountains, and swimming

Getting there: From Ketchum, drive north on Highway 75 for 18.5 miles to Prairie Creek Road. There is a big turn-off next to the highway on the left. Park, the ride begins here. (**FYI:** You could also drive to the parking area at the end of Prairie Creek Road and begin there, saving 2.6 miles.)

Miles and Directions

0.0   Begin by riding up Prairie Creek Road, which is both gravel and dirt and well-traveled in the summertime.

2.6   Reach the trailhead for Prairie Lake and continue on with singletrack from this point just after crossing the creek. Buckle down and prepare for a continuous but moderate climb.

4.9   After some fun cruising up the valley and some gradual climbing, Minor Lake Trail takes off on the left. Stay straight on the main trail up toward Prairie Lake, but make a note; this is where you will rejoin the trail later.

6.8   Encounter a small meadow with the creek running through it. Stay on the right side and cross over the creek at the upper end of the meadow and continue on to the lake.

7.2   Prairie Lake. Great swimming on the eastern side next to the trail. Careful of the creek flowing in; it's freezing! Look for the trail leading to the left and northeast away from the lake area. It should have a sign pointing to Miner Lake. Follow this trail as it mostly contours and climbs (approximately 600 feet) over to Miner Lake.

8.8   Do NOT take the first left at what you will think is the trail leading back down the valley. Go another 25 yards and turn left at the main trail junction.

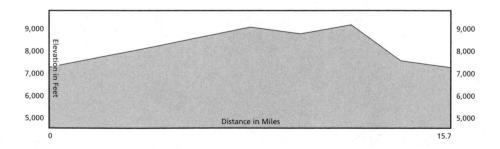

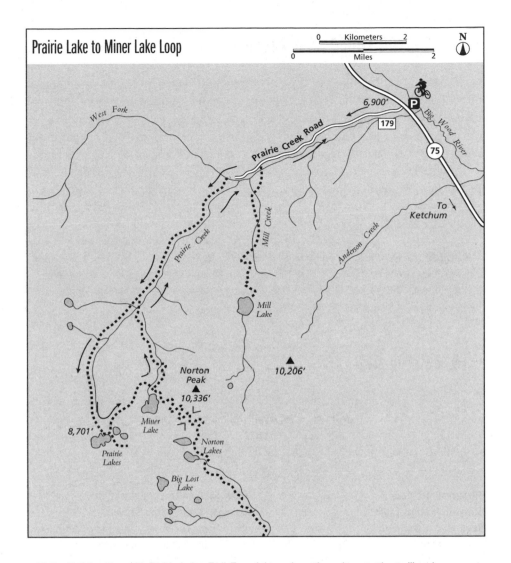

10.8 Trail junction with Prairie Lakes Trail. Turn right and continue down to the trailhead.

13.1 The Prairie Lake Trailhead. If you parked here, have a nice drive out; otherwise, continue down the road to your car at Highway 75.

15.7 End of the ride.

38 Galena Lodge Area Rides

Galena Lodge has been around since 1974 as a cross-country skiing and mountain bike/hiking center. Since mountain biking and other outdoor recreation pursuits have increased in popularity over the years, the lodge has taken an aggressive move in creating a great trail network. With old mines and pioneer cabins throughout the area, any ride at Galena Lodge Area is a great time. The trails at Galena are all pieces of a puzzle known as the Galena Grinder, a local race utilizing nearly all of the trails in one form or another. Maps are available at the lodge for all trails, and the trails are well-marked. Go up, have a great time, and enjoy a lunch or dinner on the deck in the heart of the Boulder Mountains.

Getting there: From Ketchum, drive north on Highway 75 for 24 miles until you see the GALENA LODGE sign and lodge on the right side of the road. Turn right into the parking lot to begin your fun. If you reach Galena Summit, you've gone too far, but will have an awesome view of the Sawtooth and Boulder Mountains in return.

38a Galena Trail

Starting with a cruiser up the Senate Meadow, you then climb up the jeep road to a singletrack trail traversing the mountains all the way down into the gulch by the corrals after passing straight through the gravel pit. From here, the trail climbs up and over the hill down into Gladiator Meadow and back to Galena Lodge.

Distance: 10 miles
Difficulty rating: Difficult
Technical rating: 2+
The ride: Loop
Starting elevation: 7,290 feet
High point elevation: 8,200 feet
Total elevation gain: 1,090 feet

Surface: Singletrack and jeep road
Season: June through September
Fun factor: Locals have put many hard hours into making this one of the more classic rides in the upper valley area. Incredible views, climbs, and downhills await you!

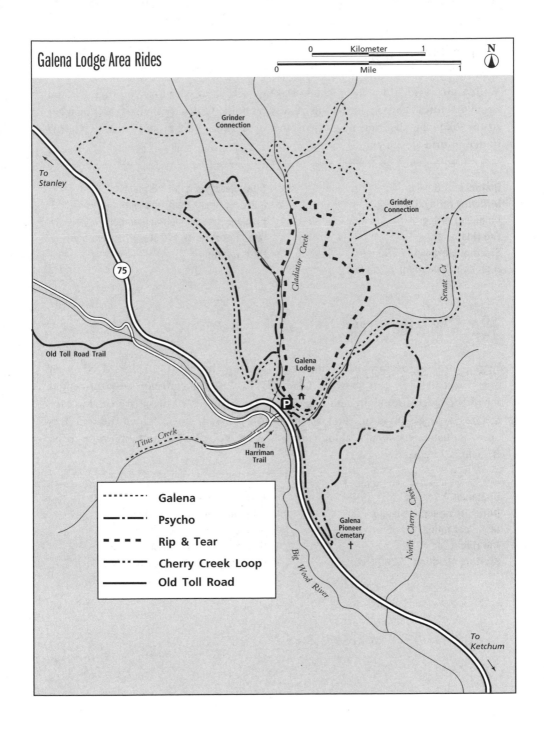

Galena Lodge Area Rides

0 Kilometer 1
0 Mile 1

N

To Stanley

75

Old Toll Road Trail

Grinder Connection

Grinder Connection

Gladiator Creek

Senate Cr

Galena Lodge

P

Titus Creek

The Harriman Trail

Galena Pioneer Cematery

North Cherry Creek

Big Wood River

To Ketchum

- - - - - - - - Galena
- · - · - · Psycho
- - - - Rip & Tear
- ·· - ·· - Cherry Creek Loop
━━━━━ Old Toll Road

38b Psycho Trail

With a nice gradual warm-up riding through Gladiator Meadow, you turn left and begin a gradual climb up to the top of Westernhome Gulch. From here, you turn left again, following the ridgeline, down and up Emma's Gulch and back to Galena Lodge in time for lunch.

Distance: 4.8 miles
Difficulty rating: Difficult
Technical rating: 2
The ride: Loop
Starting elevation: 7,290 feet
High point elevation: 7,750 feet

Total elevation gain: 460 feet
Surface: Single track and jeep road
Season: June through September
Fun factor: Quick and steep (not too bad)—a great warm-up

38c Rip & Tear Trail

Begin with another gradually climbing warm-up through Gladiator Meadow. At the Forest Service sign showing Gladiator Pass (straight ahead), you turn right across the creek and begin climbing. As you crest the top of the jeep road, look for the singletrack peeling off right on the nordic ski trail. This is where the trail lives up to its name, eventually taking riders by some yurts before dumping them back at Galena Lodge.

Distance: 4.5 miles
Difficulty rating: Moderate
Technical rating: 2
The ride: Loop
Starting elevation: 7,290 feet

High point elevation: 7,800 feet
Total elevation gain: 510 feet
Surface: Singletrack and jeep road
Season: June through September
Fun factor: Another short but sweet loop

38d Cherry Creek Loop

Ride up Senate Meadow on the main road leading right. As the road tops out, a singletrack spur descends to the right, eventually making its way back to the road. Soon after, you will plunge down North Cherry Creek, go left and climb approximately 1,000 feet back to the top of the loop. You can then either go left to the lodge, or go right and connect onto Galena Loop.

Distance: 4 miles
Difficulty rating: Easy
Technical rating: 2
The ride: Loop
Starting elevation: 7,290 feet
High point elevation: 7,600 feet
Total elevation gain: 310 feet

Surface: Singletrack and jeep road
Season: June through September
Fun factor: Although mainly a jeep road, this ride will definitely challenge your climbing ability and put you in one of the most beautiful areas around Galena.

38e Old Toll Road

Access from Galena Lodge or the top of Galena Pass. From the lodge, follow Northwood Trail to the end and go left where it meets the highway. Go left and climb up to the top of the pass.

Distance: Approximately 4 miles to the top
Difficulty rating: Moderate
Technical rating: 2+
The ride: Out-and-back (or loop with the highway)
Starting elevation: 7,290 feet

High point elevation: 8,700 feet
Total elevation gain: 1,410 feet
Surface: Singletrack
Season: June through September
Fun factor: Some of the most amazing views of the entire valley

Riding in the Stanley Area

When you make the trek up to Stanley, you enter into another world of amazing beauty, abundant wildlife, and incredible trails. The Sawtooth Mountains will demand much of your attention as you drive into the area, making you want to stay and play for longer than intended.

Some places not to miss in the area are Redfish Lake Lodge for cocktails lakeside or just a nice refreshing dip in the lake. The Smiley Creek Lodge has a great deck for post-ride milkshakes or pre-ride munchies. However, if it's atmosphere, people, and amazing food you're after, do not miss the Stanley Baking Company in the heart of Stanley (on the way to the airport!). If you need any outdoor gear or bike supplies while in the area, you can visit Riverwear, which carries most all bike parts you could possibly need and then some.

Camping in the Stanley area can get crowded at some of the more popular areas, so feel free to jump into primitive camping mode and hit any dirt road leading off the beaten path. You just won't have a toilet or shower, no biggie.

Basically, get out and have some fun all around the area. There's hiking, biking, swimming, rafting, kayaking, hunting, fishing, and picnicking to be had around every corner. Stanley is truly an undiscovered gem of the West. Help us to keep it a special place for everyone to enjoy.

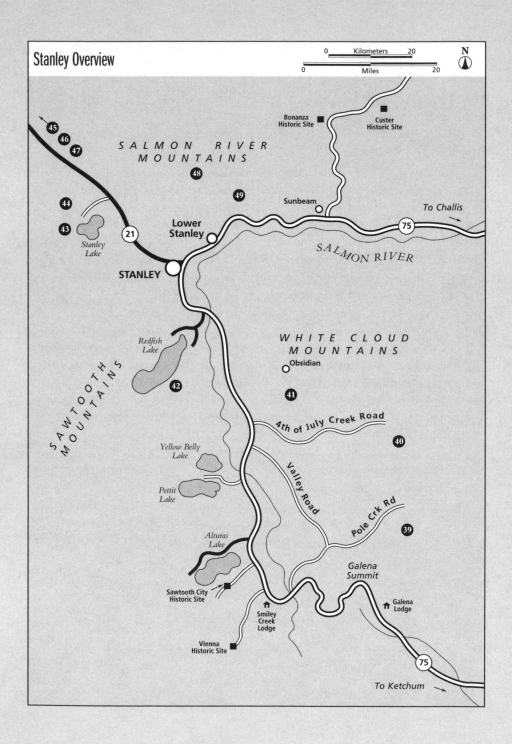

Stanley Overview

Kilometers
Miles

N

SALMON RIVER MOUNTAINS

Bonanza Historic Site
Custer Historic Site

45
46
47

48

49

Sunbeam

75   To Challis

44

43

Stanley Lake

21

Lower Stanley

STANLEY

SALMON RIVER

Redfish Lake

WHITE CLOUD MOUNTAINS

Obsidian

42

41

SAWTOOTH MOUNTAINS

4th of July Creek Road

40

Yellow Belly Lake

Pettit Lake

Valley Road

Pole Crk Rd

39

Alturas Lake

Galena Summit

Sawtooth City Historic Site

Smiley Creek Lodge

Galena Lodge

Vienna Historic Site

75

To Ketchum

39 The Bowery Loop

You'll feel good at the top of Grand Prize Gulch; you'll even feel good by the time you reach Bowery. But by the time you reach the top of the hike-a-bike, you'll be praying to the endurance gods for forgiveness. The rest is a classic wilderness ride.

Distance: 30.5 miles
Difficulty rating: Abusive
Technical rating: 4
The ride: Loop
Starting elevation: 7,760 feet
High point elevation: 9,060 feet

Total elevation gain: 4,670 feet
Surface: Dirt jeep road and singletrack
Season: July through September
Fun factor: Remote wilderness area with views and serious wildlife . . . be prepared!

Getting there: From Ketchum, drive north on Highway 75 for just over 37 miles and turn right at the POLE CREEK ROAD AND VALLEY ROAD sign. (If you go flying past the Smiley Creek Lodge, you've just gone 0.5 mile too far.) If coming from Stanley, go south on Highway 75 for just over 24.5 miles and turn left at the same sign. Stay on the main road heading toward the mountains, passing several spur roads along the way. At 2.3 miles, you cross over Pole Creek and come to a junction. Continue forward on the road heading toward Germania Basin. The left fork becomes Valley Road. Follow this road for another 4.2 miles until Grand Prize Gulch appears on the right. The ride begins and ends here.

Miles and Directions

0.0 Begin by finding the trail that crosses over Pole Creek. Just after crossing the creek, be sure to take the left fork 0.3 mile later.

1.5 The road ends at the creek crossing and becomes singletrack.

2.9 The switchbacks end in high alpine meadows.

3.7 Just after the main saddle, Gladiator Trail takes off on the right.

9.0 Small junction with the West Fork and South Fork. Stay on the main trail.

11.4 Cross by sign for Ibex Creek Canyon on the right.

12.6 A small trail takes off to the left. Both trails get to the same place, but stay right and cross the creek.

13.4 Gate: Please close.

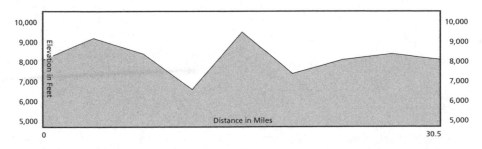

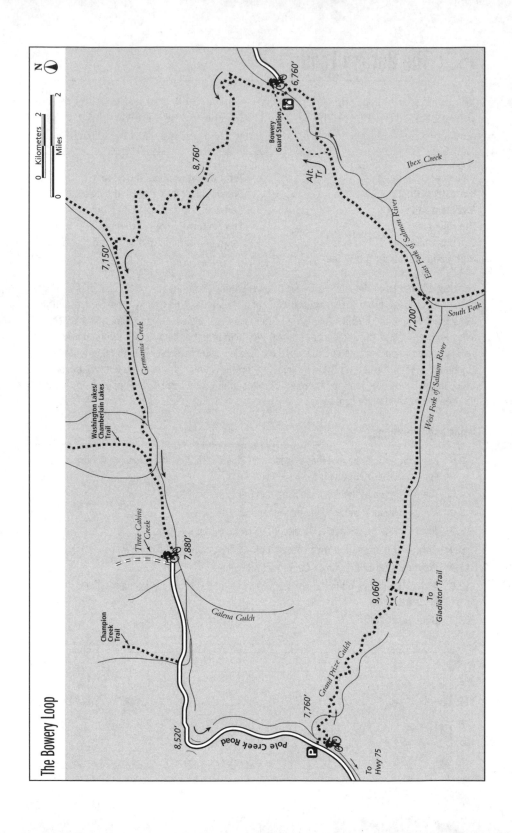

The Bowery Loop

N

0 Kilometers 2
0 Miles 2

8,760'

7,150'

Germania Creek

Washington Lakes/
Chamberlain Lakes
Trail

Three Cabins
Creek

7,880'

Champion
Creek
Trail

Galena Gulch

8,520'

Pole Creek Road

To
Hwy 75

P

7,760'

Grand Prize Gulch

9,060'

To
Gladiator Trail

West Fork of Salmon River

7,200'

South Fork

East Fork of Salmon River

Ibex Creek

Bowery Guard Station

6,760'

Alt.
Tr.

13.6 Take the very faint trail that cuts back to the left just when the guard station comes into view. Follow this trail down to the bridge that crosses over the creek by the guard station. Go through the guard station courtyard area to the gate against the hill on the west side. Close the gate behind you and go right.

14.0 Another gate crossing: Keep traversing the hillside before starting the hike-a-bike climbing section in the aspen trees ahead of you.

14.6 The climbing seriously begins now; either push, carry, or cry.

16.6 Yes! This is the top, nice job! Scramble up the 9,059-foot peak on the right for killer views of Castle Peak. Careful going down from here; it is seriously loose, steep, and dangerous. If you get hurt here, you are a long ways from help!

18.8 The trail intersects Germania Creek, stay left.

19.7 Cross the creek here, anywhere you can, and continue riding left and up.

23.2 Junction with Washington Lakes/Chamberlain Lakes Trail. Stay on main trail.

24.7 End of the singletrack and junction with Pole Creek Road. Ride up road.

27.8 The top of Pole Creek Summit. It's all downhill from here!

30.5 Back at your car and the end of the ride.

40 Fourth of July to Pole Creek

Let's say you want one hell of a long ride, some serious uphill with a backcountry commitment that takes the better part of a day. This is the ride for you! It's gorgeous and you get into areas where not many others go.

Distance: 38.1 miles
Difficulty rating: Difficult/Abusive
Technical rating: 3
The ride: Loop
Starting elevation: 6,800 feet
High point elevation: 9,580 feet

Total elevation gain: 2,780 feet
Surface: Dirt road and singletrack trail
Season: June through October
Fun factor: Alpine lakes, great descending, and fun climbing

Getting there: From Ketchum, drive north 47 miles on Highway 75 over Galena Summit past Smiley Creek Lodge to Fourth of July Creek Road. Turn right here and park anywhere in the sage

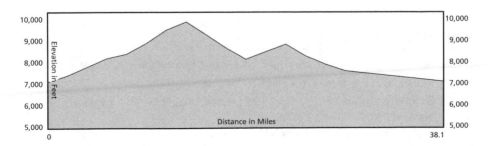

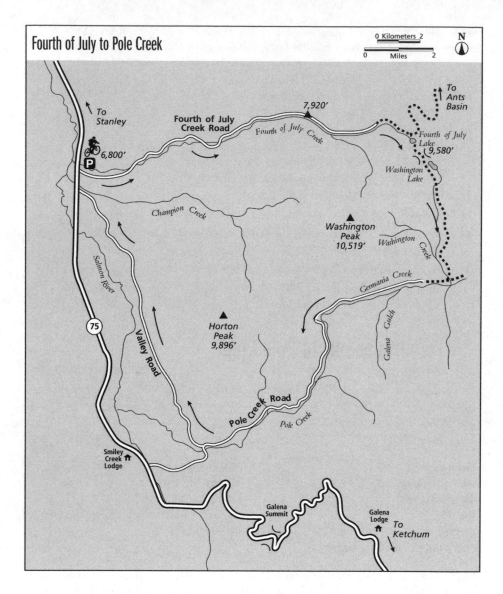

0 Kilometers 2

N

0   Miles   2

To
Stanley

6,800'

P

Fourth of July
Creek Road

Fourth of July Creek

7,920'

To
Ants
Basin

Fourth of July
Lake
9,580'

Washington
Lake

Champion Creek

Washington
Peak
10,519'

Washington Creek

Germania Creek

Salmon River

75

Valley Road

Horton
Peak
9,896'

Galena Gulch

Pole Creek Road

Pole Creek

Smiley
Creek
Lodge

Galena
Summit

Galena
Lodge

To
Ketchum

by the road. You're approximately 15 miles from Stanley, heading south on Highway 75. The ride begins here.

Miles and Directions

0.0   Begin by riding up the dirt/gravel road heading east toward the White Cloud Mountains.

1.0   Pass by the Fourth of July Creek Ranch on the right.

1.7   Enter in the trees by the creek. From here, the road winds while climbing gradually through the trees following the creek.

4.1   Cabin ruins and white cliffs on the left.

4.8 Pass by Champion Creek trailhead on the right.

8.3 A primitive campground on the right marks the beginning of more aggressive climbing to come. Gear down.

9.2 A slight break from climbing in the meadows.

10.3 Trailhead. Please register to make the USFS happy. From here, follow the singletrack trail to the two lakes ahead.

11.8 Trail junction. The left fork leads over the saddle and into Warm Springs Creek, eventually joining up with Fisher Creek (very adventurous). Instead, take the right (forward) fork and come to Fourth of July Lake just ahead of you. From here, continue on to the lake and up the trail to the saddle with Washington Lake.

12.8 You've reached Washington Lake. Continue on the trail as it descends into Germania Creek.

13.6 At the fork, turn right heading toward Germania Creek, where it climbs a short bit before becoming more mellow 0.5 mile later.

15.9 At the fork, turn left and down toward Germania Creek, heading toward the junction of Germania and Washington Creeks.

16.7 Another fork. Stay straight (right) and continue riding down a steep section into Germania Creek.

17.6 Trail junction. Join Germania Creek Trail and turn right here, climbing slightly up to the main road.

18.9 Germania Creek trailhead. Follow the road up and out for the next 3 miles, ascending the upper Germania Creek drainage.

22.1 The top of Pole Creek summit.

28.6 Whoa! At the junction, be careful not to miss the right turn here leading up the small hill on Valley Road. Continue on Valley Road all the way to Highway 75, cruising down the east side of the Salmon River basin.

37.6 End of Valley Road and junction with Highway 75. Turn right here and continue heading north down Highway 75 to Fourth of July Creek Road.

38.1 Turn right on Fourth of July Creek Road and return to your car. This is the end of an amazing ride.

41 Fisher Creek

When you have the time and the desire for a ride that you'll be talking about for years to come, this is it. Great climbing, stream crossings, and a descent that would make anyone jealous; it's all right here waiting for you. (**Note:** In the fall of 2005 this entire area was severely burned by a forest fire. You will come across moonscapes, burned trees, and incredible views. Please do not ride around fallen trees; instead, lift your bike over them and do your part in preventing erosion.)

Distance: 17.8 miles
Difficulty rating: Moderate/Difficult
Technical rating: 2
The ride: Loop
Starting elevation: 6,625 feet
High point elevation: 8,125 feet

Total elevation gain: 1,500 feet
Surface: Pavement, dirt jeep road, and single-track trail
Season: June through October
Fun factor: The ultimate ride!!

Getting there: From Ketchum, drive north on Highway 75 up and over Galena Summit, passing by Smiley Creek Store and Sessions Lodge, to the Williams Creek trailhead at just over 50 miles from Ketchum. If coming from Stanley, drive south on Highway 75 for approximately 13.5 miles to the turn-off. The parking area is on the east side of the highway. Park here and gear up.

Miles and Directions

0.0 Begin by riding up the highway (south), back toward the direction you just came from.

2.3 Turn left onto Fisher Creek Road and begin a gradual cruise up the road for 6.5 miles.

8.4 Begin a very rideable climb, which tops out after 0.33 mile. Don't worry if you have to push your bike for a few feet. This is the only place in the ride you'll have to.

9.1 You're at the top. Please register yourself so the USFS can keep tabs on the number of riders/hikers per year, and get ready for the ultimate in downhill pleasure. Be sure to take the singletrack trail leading west off this saddle.

10.6 Fork in the trail. Take the left fork and continue on the Fisher Creek Loop, which gradually winds and climbs its way up the small valley. The right fork leads to Warm Springs Meadow.

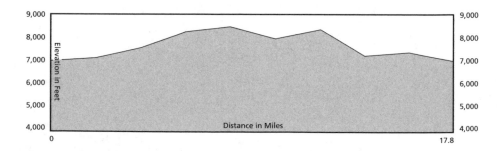

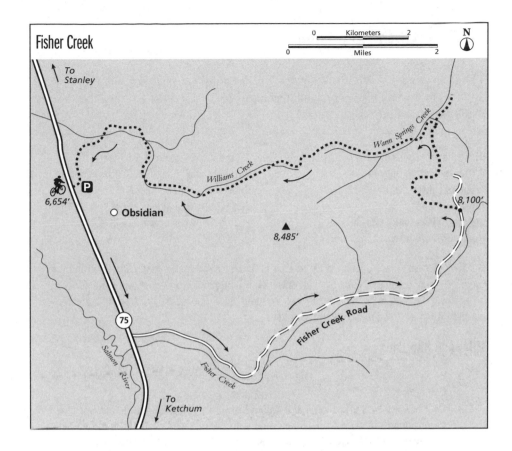

12.7 Another saddle. From here, be careful and enjoy the bobsled descent for the next 3+ miles.

16.0 Cross over the bridge/creek and into a pristine meadow for a little regrouping. Continue left and up toward a small switchback (all rideable) and begin a fairly small climb.

16.4 Top of the last climb and only descending lies ahead. Be sure to take in the view of the Sawtooths in the last clearing before the end of the ride—know where I mean.

17.8 End of the ride at Williams Creek trailhead.

42 Redfish Lake Loop

The loop around Redfish Lake may seem like a little afternoon jaunt, but don't let the map fool you. This is a difficult, technical ride that'll make you beg the campers at the far end of the lake for food.

Distance: 13.9 miles
Difficulty rating: Difficult
Technical rating: 3
The ride: Loop
Starting elevation: 6,550 feet
High point elevation: 7,560 feet

Total elevation gain: 1,940 feet
Surface: singletrack trail and pavement
Season: Mid-June through October
Fun factor: Beautiful views of White Cloud Mountains, wildlife, and the lake

Getting there: From Ketchum, drive north on Highway 75 to the Redfish Lake Road turn-off (approximately 55 miles). From Stanley, drive south on Highway75 for just over 4 miles. At 2 miles down the road pass the REDFISH LODGE sign and junction on the right. A parking area is on the right just past this junction. Park/start here.

Miles and Directions

0.0 Begin by riding out of the parking area heading south on the paved road toward Sockeye Campground.

1.6 After passing by Sandy Beach and Mount Heyburn Campground, turn into Sockeye Campground and go left (the wrong way) onto the one-way road. Turn left onto the singletrack Trail 045 (you'll see the DECKER FLATS sign), and pass behind the campground bathrooms.

2.1 Begin a gradual roller-coaster climb with some steeps here and there.

3.1 Gain the summit ridge and check out the beautiful views of the Sawtooths, Stanley basin, and Redfish Lake. Please watch for horses in this section.

3.3 ELK MEADOW sign on left. Stay straight on the main trail.

4.0 DECKER FLATS TRAIL 400 sign on left. Stay on main trail along the ridge.

5.9 At the signed junction, turn right and down towards the lake.

7.8 A very techy section; be careful of the wet rocks and logs close to the lake.

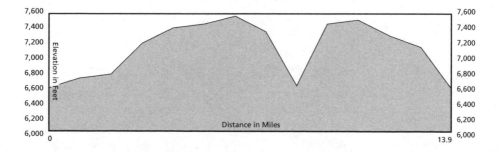

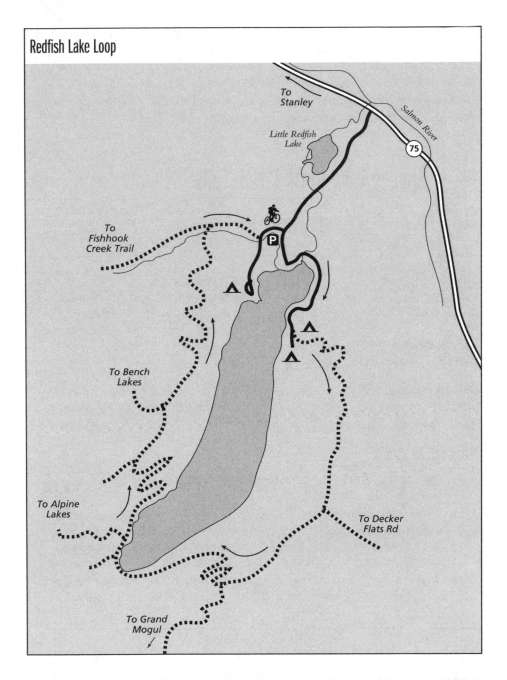

Redfish Lake Loop

To Stanley

Salmon River

Little Redfish Lake

75

To Fishhook Creek Trail

P

To Bench Lakes

To Alpine Lakes

To Decker Flats Rd

To Grand Mogul

8.0 Trail junction. Stay right on main trail or hike on the left trail to some falls.

8.2 In a tree'd and washy area look for the bridge crossing the creek and follow that trail around and behind Inlet Campground. Follow this trail along the fence next to the campground, then you will start to ride away from the campground along the lake.

9.4 Trail junction. At the switchback, stay right and continue climbing up.

10.6 Just past the top of the climbing is a trail junction. The left trail leads to Bench Lakes. Stay along the ridge on the main trail heading down.

13.5 Trail junction. Stay right and down along Fishhook Creek. Shortly afterward, a small trail leads to the left to the Redfish Corrals; don't go there either.

13.8 Cross over the paved road and continue to the parking area.

13.9 The parking area, your car, and the end of another epic, fun ride!

43 Stanley Lake to Bridalveil Falls

This ride can give you views, waterfalls, the Sawtooth Mountains, and a lake to swim in.

Distance: 14.2 miles
Difficulty rating: Easy/Moderate
Technical rating: 2
The ride: Out-and-back
Starting elevation: 6,350 feet
High point elevation: 7,400 feet

Total elevation gain: 1,050 feet
Surface: Gravel road, singletrack trail
Season: June through September
Fun factor: Gorgeous views of the Sawtooth Mountains

Getting there: From Stanley, drive west on Highway 21 for 5 miles and park on the left side of the road at the beginning of Stanley Lake Road 455. The ride begins here. You can also just drive up the road to the lake and forget potential traffic.

Miles and Directions

0.0 Begin by riding west on Stanley Lake Road. Climb slowly through the forest; be sure to stay on the main road to the lake.

3.5 Go left on the road heading toward the boat launch and pass by Inlet Campground. Ride to the end of the turn-around and turn right toward the Alpine Way trailhead. From here, the trail is a nice raised gravelly trail over water-logged areas. Great for strollers, bike trailers, etc., until the dirt climbing ahead, which is where the trail picks up in steepness and fun!

4.8 Alpine Way Trail goes off to the left and enters the Sawtooth Wilderness Area. The SWA is off-limits to mountain bikes, but a great place for a hike on another day. Continue on

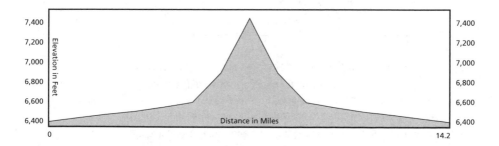

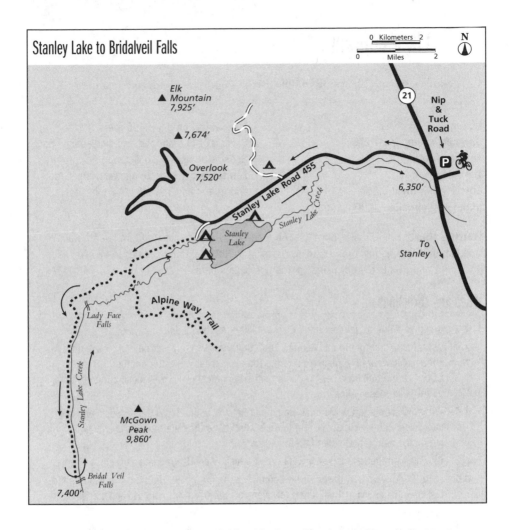

Elk
▲ Mountain
7,925'

▲ 7,674'

Overlook
7,520'

Stanley Lake Road 455

Stanley Lake Creek

Stanley
Lake

21

Nip
&
Tuck
Road

P

6,350'

To
Stanley

Alpine Way Trail

Lady Face
Falls

Stanley Lake Creek

McGown
Peak
9,860'

Bridal Veil
Falls

7,400'

N

0 Kilometers 2

0   Miles   2

and stay straight on the main trail. After this, the trail levels out a bit and roller-coasters through the forest. You'll eventually see two trails (one after the other) leading off to the right going to the falls. Take a picture, be careful, and watch out for slippery rocks!

7.1   Trail junction and the top of the ride. Take the trail to the right to go check out Bridalveil Falls. The left fork enters the SWA again. Turn around here and enjoy the ride back down to your car. If you continue on up the trail, be prepared for some serious hike-a-bike that isn't really very enjoyable.

14.2   End of the ride.

44 Elk Mountain

Gorgeous views and plenty of wildlife. Bring bug juice, food, and a camera.

Distance: 12.4 miles
Difficulty rating: Moderate
Technical rating: 2
The ride: Loop
Starting elevation: 6,550 feet
High point elevation: 7,000 feet

Total elevation gain: 450 feet
Surface: Dirt jeep road and singletrack trail
Season: June through October
Fun factor: Wildlife, wildflowers, rocks, roots, and mountains. You will LOVE this ride!

Getting there: From Stanley, drive west on Highway 21 for 5 miles and turn left on Stanley Lake Road 455. Drive just over 3.5 miles (passing by the Inlet Campground) to Elk Mountain Road 649 and park in the day-use area. The ride begins here.

Miles and Directions

0.0 Begin by riding up Elk Mountain Road, which is a gradual grind up.

1.8 Whoa! Look left for the Elk Meadow Loop trailhead and turn left here. If you want a real grind, continue up the main road to the top for a great view after another 1.3 miles and 600 feet. The trail from here becomes rather technical going over rocks and tree roots, all the while descending.

3.5 Whoa! Welcome to Elk Meadow. Be careful not to continue into the meadow and get inundated with skeeters, elk, and mud. Instead, take the faint trail to the right while staying on the right (east) side of the meadow.

5.2 Turn right on the trail paralleling Elk Creek, which ascends gradually through the trees.

6.5 Continue forward and down, slowly contouring the mountain. Hold on; this is some fun, fast downhill cruising! There are a few signs on the trail from here to keep you going the right way.

9.8 Trail junction. Go right and shortly thereafter, up the small hill.

11.2 After cruising through a camping area, join Stanley Lake Road. Go right and follow the road back to your car at the day-use area.

12.4 Back at your car and the end of the ride.

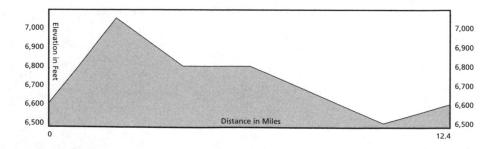

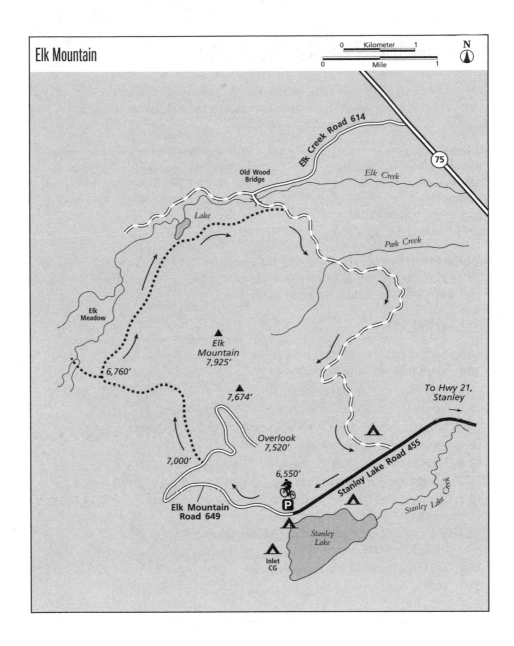

Elk Mountain

0 Kilometer 1
0 Mile 1

N

Elk Creek Road 614

75

Old Wood Bridge

Elk Creek

Lake

Park Creek

Elk Meadow

Elk Mountain 7,925'

6,760'

7,674'

Overlook 7,520'

To Hwy 21, Stanley

7,000'

6,550'

Stanley Lake Road 455

Elk Mountain Road 649

Stanley Lake Creek

P

Stanley Lake

Inlet CG

45 Valley Creek-Knapp Creek Loop

This is a ride you will remember at least 'til the next one. Actually, this is a modified ATV trail that kicks some serious mountain biking butt! It is mellow and fun!

Distance: 21.1 miles
Difficulty rating: Easy/Moderate
Technical rating: 1+
The ride: Loop
Starting elevation: 6,647 feet
High point elevation: 7,290 feet

Total elevation gain: 643 feet
Surface: Dirt jeep road and singletrack trail
Season: June through October
Fun factor: Elk, beautiful meadows, killer trail, and mountains

Getting there: From Stanley, drive west on Highway 21 for 11.1 miles and turn right on Road 203. At 11.9 miles, you'll pass the BLIND SUMMIT sign, and at 14.3 miles, turn right and park close to the VALLEY CREEK TRAILHEAD sign. The ride starts here.

Miles and Directions

0.0 Begin by continuing up the road toward the Valley Creek trailhead.

0.9 At the obvious junction, stay to the left.

1.6 Another junction. Stay to the right here.

2.4 Yet another junction. Stay right here, too.

3.1 Ah, finally, the Valley Creek trailhead. Seriously, it gets incredible from here!

7.3 Here you encounter a small climb.

7.8 Prospect Creek is on the right. Stay straight.

8.6 Trail junction. Go left toward Cape Horn Guard Station and Knapp Creek.

9.2 Big creek crossing over Knapp Creek, followed by another major trail junction. Take a left here toward the Cape Horn Guard Station.

11.4 Stay left at the junction and continue following Knapp Creek down. The trail leading off to the right goes to Winnemucca Creek.

14.5 The Knapp Creek trailhead. Follow the gravel-dirt road down to the Cape Horn Guard Station.

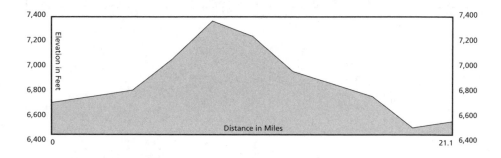

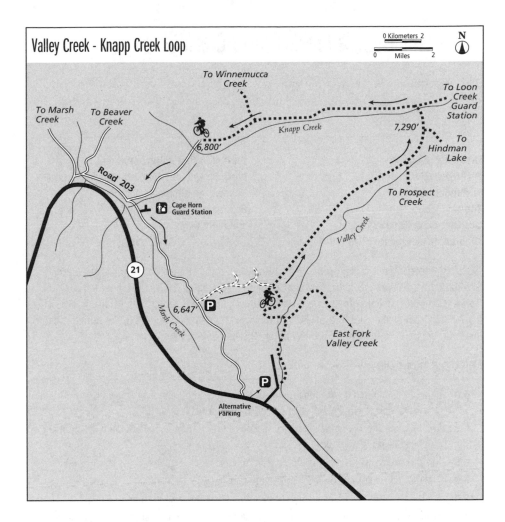

Valley Creek - Knapp Creek Loop

18.6 At USFS 203 (the first main road), stay left and start looking for elk grazing in the evenings and mornings.

19.3 Pass by the Cape Horn Guard Station on the left.

21.1 Hey look! Is that your car? If so, the ride is over. If not, you're lost. Refer to the map for more information. Now pay attention next time, huh?

46 Winnemucca Creek-Beaver Creek Loop

This is another ride you will remember at least 'til the next one and another modified ATV trail that is seriously fun! Aside from the few climbs it is fairly mellow and extremely gorgeous.

Distance: 13.4 miles
Difficulty rating: Moderate
Technical rating: 2+
The ride: Loop
Starting elevation: 6,850 feet
High point elevation: 7,900 feet

Total elevation gain: 1,050 feet
Surface: Dirt jeep road and singletrack trail
Season: June through October
Fun factor: Elk, beautiful meadows, killer trail, and mountains

Getting there: From Stanley, drive west on Highway 21 for 18 miles and turn right into the Seafoam Area. As the road forks, stay right again immediately. At 18.5 miles, bear left toward Beaver Creek Campground. Then at 23.8 miles, turn right toward Loon Creek Guard Station. At 26.7 miles from Stanley and 8.3 miles from Highway 21, park on the right in the primitive camping area just before crossing over Beaver Creek. The ride begins here.

Miles and Directions

0.0 Begin by continuing up the main road you just came in on and over Beaver Creek. After a little climb and 0.1 mile, turn right toward Winnemucca Creek.

0.8 Trail junction. The right fork leads over to Knapp Creek, but instead continue on the main trail heading up Winnemucca Creek.

5.5 The trail begins to gradually climb a bit from here.

6.0 A short, steep climb followed by more gradual climbing.

6.5 Ah, the top of the climbing portion of the ride. It's all downhill from here!

7.2 At the short marshy area, please be cautious of eroding the trail any more than it already is. After this, you encounter a short, steep hill followed immediately by a crossing of Beaver Creek.

7.8 Trail junction. Stay left here and continue down the trail descending Beaver Creek.

9.5 Trail junction with Beaver Creek Trail. Stay left and continue down.

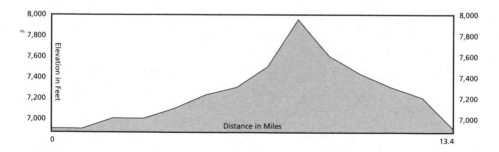

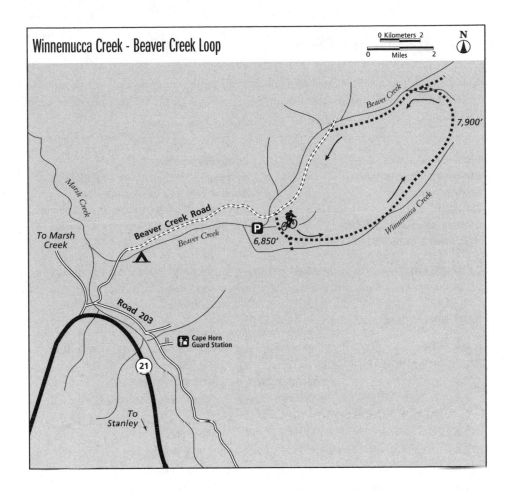

9.8 The singletrack trail ends at Beaver Creek Road. Stay left here and cruise down the road toward your car.

13.4 Ah, the end of the ride and your car (hopefully!).

47 Wyoming Creek

You go from pavement to jeep road and then to singletrack, working you from start to finish. You will be tired, thirsty, and hungry for more. This is an amazing adventure ride!

Distance: 27.7 miles
Difficulty rating: Difficult
Technical rating: 3+
The ride: Loop
Starting elevation: 6,980 feet
High point elevation: 8,400 feet

Total elevation gain: 2,360 feet
Surface: Dirt jeep road and singletrack trail
Season: Mid-June through October
Fun factor: You will be in an area that most people only dream of seeing.

Getting there: From Stanley, drive west on Highway 21 for 24.2 miles and park on the right in the pull-out just past the turn to Bull Trout Lake. The ride begins here.

Miles and Directions

0.0 Begin by riding back down Highway 21 for 2.8 miles and turn left onto Boundary Creek Road and ride to the summit.

5.9 The top of Boundary Creek Road. Go down and stay on the main road.

8.3 Fir Creek Trail takes off to the left; stay on the road. This trail actually intersects Wyoming Creek Trail near its summit.

11.4 Enter into Bruce Meadows and go by the landing strip shortly.

12.5 Rest area. Stay on the main road heading south toward Wyoming Creek.

13.6 Turn left on Wyoming Creek Road, just after a left-side spur road.

14.4 The official Wyoming Creek trailhead. Follow the singletrack trail.

18.8 Junction with Fir Creek Trail on the left. Continue up Wyoming Creek Trail.

19.0 The top of the climbing and 8,400 feet.

20.5 Enter into the burned-out matchstick forest. Watch for sandy soil.

22.0 The trail goes up and over the ridge in a sort of hike-a-bike . . . it's quick!

22.6 The top of the ridge. It's all downhill from here!

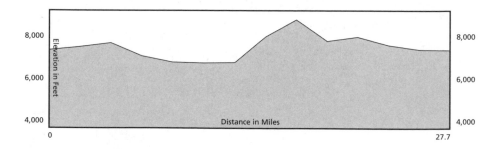

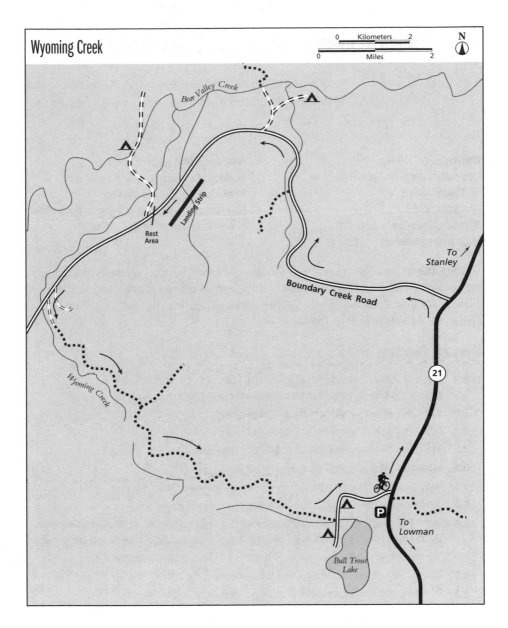

24.7 Trail junction with the main trail leading toward the Bull Trout Lake area. Stay on the main trail and into the parking area. Then follow that road back out to Highway 21.

27.7 Junction with Highway 21. Turn right and your car should be right there on the shoulder. End of the ride.

48 Potato Mountain Loop (Little Basin Creek)

This is destined to be another Fisher Creek ride someday. Get there before the crowds do. Amazing downhills, fun climbs, and if you bonk, the wolves will take care of you. Just kidding.

Distance: 14.3 miles
Difficulty rating: Moderate
Technical rating: 2+
The ride: Loop
Starting elevation: 6,600 feet
High point elevation: 7,450 feet

Total elevation gain: 1,250 feet
Surface: Dirt jeep road and singletrack
Season: June through October
Fun factor: The feeling of being in the middle of nowhere, but you're not . . . really.

Getting there: From Stanley, drive west on Highway 21 for 5 miles to Stanley Creek Road. Turn right and go 1.4 miles to a big brown map board. Go left. At the next junction, just over the creek, go right and follow this road for 2.9 miles (total mileage from Highway 21 is 4.3 miles). Park on the right in the clearing. The ride begins here.

Miles and Directions

0.0 Begin by riding up Road 653. At the mining ruins at 0.4 mile, stay to the right and against the hillside on the doubletrack jeep trail.

1.0 Cross over Stanley Creek and the fun really begins.

2.0 The climbing begins and eases off a short distance later.

2.5 Top of the climbing. The downhill begins into Little Basin Creek . . . yeehaa!

2.8 Enter into a gigantic meadow. Careful of the elk!

3.6 Junction with Little Basin Creek. Follow the singletrack downhill from here.

5.6 After the luge-style downhill, be careful of the boulder field.

7.0 Major Trail junction. After crossing over Basin Creek, go right at the junction and descend Basin Creek Trail. If you were to go left, you would be on the Hay Creek-Knapp Creek Trail.

7.4 Big crossing of Basin Creek. We looked; there is NO alternative to getting wet.

8.1 Take the switchbacks up and around the muddy bog. It's a quick climb.

9.1 Pass by a trail leading up and left into Hay Creek. Stay on the main trail.

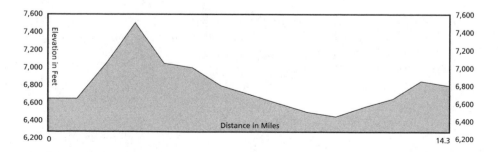

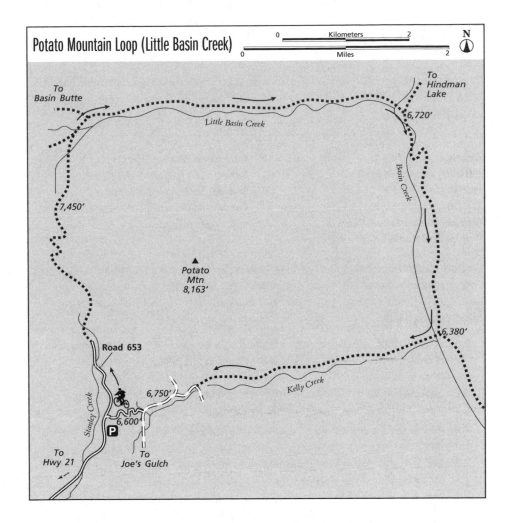

Potato Mountain Loop (Little Basin Creek)

To Basin Butte

To Hindman Lake

6,720'

Little Basin Creek

Basin Creek

7,450'

▲
Potato
Mtn
8,163'

6,380'

Road 653

Stanley Creek

6,750'

Kelly Creek

6,600'

P

To Hwy 21

To Joe's Gulch

10.6 In the large meadow, look for the KELLY CREEK sign. Cross Basin Creek here and begin a casual ride up Kelly Creek.

12.3 At the junction with the jeep road, go right and continue the casual climbing.

14.3 After a quick little descent, you're back at your car and the ride is over.

49 Basin Creek

Yet another sleepy little ride tucked away in the mountains around Stanley. This ride is a blast, roller-coasting your way up the valley on a jeep road and then to a single-track trail.

Distance: 11.4 miles
Difficulty rating: Easy
Technical rating: 1+
The ride: Out-and-back
Starting elevation: 6,050 feet
High point elevation: 6,650 feet

Total elevation gain: 600 feet
Surface: Dirt jeep road and singletrack trails
Season: June through October
Fun factor: Cruiser, whitewater, wild flowers, and wildlife

Getting there: From Stanley, drive north on Highway 75 for 8.2 miles to the Basin Creek Campground and park on the left. The ride begins here.

Miles and Directions

0.0 Begin by riding up and next to the campground on the main dirt road on the north side of Basin Creek. There is a hot spring in the creek here for some good soaking after the ride.

0.7 Spur road on the right; stay on the main road at all times.

1.1 A corral on the right is the beginning of a short climb.

2.2 After crossing over a foot bridge, the road forks. Take the left fork following Basin Creek drainage.

2.7 End of the dirt road in a big turn-around area. Follow the singletrack trail up the valley from here, roller-coastering as you go.

3.8 After crossing over a small foot bridge, there is a spur road on the right and Noho Creek on the left. Stay on the main trail heading up Basin Creek.

4.2 Kelly Creek is on the left. There is a nice singletrack trail ascending up the Kelly Creek drainage, but stay on the main trail heading up Basin Creek.

4.6 Enter into a huge meadow with a shale bridge. Pass through the meadow and please stay on the trail to prevent any unnecessary impact.

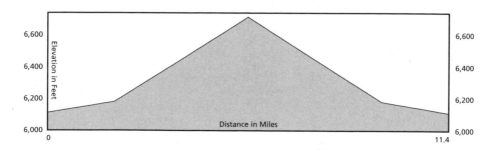

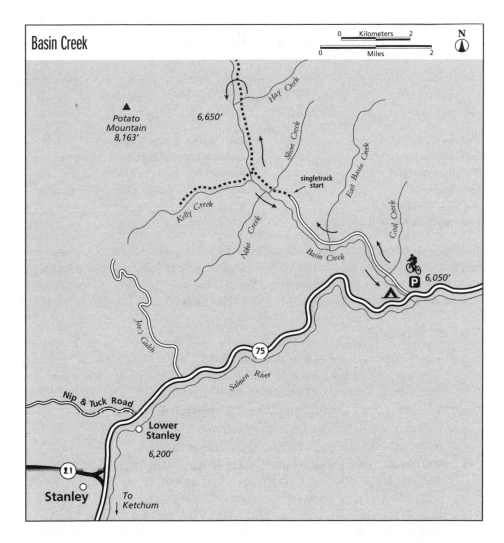

Basin Creek

Potato
Mountain
8,163'

6,650'

Hay Creek

Short Creek

singletrack
start

East Basin Creek

Coal Creek

Kelly Creek

Noho Creek

Basin Creek

6,050'

Joe's Gulch

75

Salmon River

Nip & Tuck Road

Lower
Stanley

6,200'

21

Stanley

To
Ketchum

5.7   Hay Creek Trail exits off to the right, which fades out shortly. This is the top of this ride, however, if you want to be a bit adventurous, continue on up the valley as far as you can go. Otherwise, turn around, head down and have some fun!

11.4   Back at the campground and the end of the ride.

50 Little Boulder to Big Boulder Loop

You will get worked, so prepare accordingly. Desert-like landscapes, high alpine meadows, and lakes. The downhill will freak you out it's SO good!

Distance: 24.7 miles
Difficulty rating: Difficult +
Technical rating: 4
The ride: Loop
Starting elevation: 6,100 feet
High point elevation: 9,600 feet

Total elevation gain: 4,600 feet
Surface: Dirt jeep road and singletrack trails
Season: June through October
Fun factor: Wild place with wildlife, wildflowers, and wildly amazing views

Getting there: From Stanley, drive north on Highway 75 to East Fork of Salmon River Road and turn right (thirty-minute drive). Drive 18 miles to the turn-off for Livingston Mine and park immediately on the right at the junction next to the creek. The ride begins here. (**Option:** You can also do this ride in reverse for a boulder-hopping downhill that's not to be forgotten.)

Miles and Directions

0.0 Begin by riding up East Fork of Salmon River Road.

2.8 Little Boulder Creek trailhead parking area. Ride past it on the road and turn right onto the trail about 400 yards past the parking area.

3.5 After blowing a lung at the start, the trail mellows slightly in the main canyon.

4.8 The sign-in box. Please, please, please sign your party in!

9.4 Trail junction. Turn right toward Boulder Chain Lakes and Frog Lakes.

11.4 Trail junction. Turn right toward Frog Lakes and pay no attention to the USFS sign that says it's only 1.25 miles back to the last junction . . . it's wrong.

11.8 Welcome to Frog Lakes. Watch out for the bovines.

13.8 The top of the climbing with amazing views in all directions! Wow! Now get ready for a great downhill all the way back to your car. Please watch out for hikers and backpackers, as this is a very popular route.

16.9 Pass by the turn-off to Little Redfish Lake on the right.

18.0 Trail junction. Somehow the USFS got this mileage wrong, too. Continue down the trail.

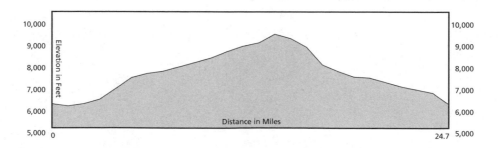

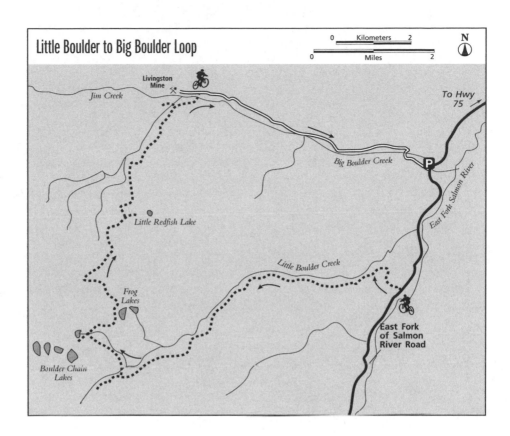

Little Boulder to Big Boulder Loop

20.3 The trailhead for Big Boulder Creek. Lots of cars and people on the weekends.

24.7 The road junction with East Fork of Salmon River Road. Hopefully your car is still there . . .

Resources (Note: The area code for the entire area is 208.)

Local Bike Shops (Service and Rental)

Ketchum
Backwoods Mountain Sports: Warm Springs Road & Main Street; 726–8818
Durance Cycleworks: 131 2nd Street; 726–7693
The Elephant's Perch: 280 East Avenue; 726–3497
Formula Sports: 460 North Main; 726–3194
Kelly Sports: Colonnade Building, Sun Valley Road; 726–8503
Pete Lanes: River Run Plaza at Bald Mountain; 622–6144
Pete Lanes: Sun Valley Village; 622-2279
Ski Tek: 191 Sun Valley Road; 726–7503
Sturtevants in Hailey: 201 North Main; 788–7847
Sturtos: 380 North Main; 726–4512
Sun Summit: 791 Warm Springs Road; 726–0707

Hailey
Sun Summit South: 418 South Main; 788–6006

Stanley
Riverwear: Highway 21; 744–3592

Local Coffee Scene

Hailey:
Hailey Coffee Company: 219 South Main
Java on Main: 310 North Main

Ketchum:
The Grinder: 4th and Leadville
Java on Fourth: 191 4th Street
Starbucks: Main Street and Sun Valley Road
Tully's: 601 Sun Valley Road

Motel/Hotel Info

Bellevue:
High Country Motel and Cabins: 765 South Main Street; 788–2050

Hailey:
Airport Inn: 820 4th Avenue South; 788–2477
Wood River Inn: 603 North Main Street; 578–0600

Ketchum:

Best Western Kentwood Lodge: 180 North Main Street; 726–4114
Clarion Inn: 600 North Main Street; 726–5601

Area Reservations:

Base Mountain Properties: 726–5601
Classic Lodging: 727–6805
Sun Valley Area Reservations: 726–3660
Sun Valley Lodge Reservations: 622–2151

General Information

Ketchum Ranger District: 622–5371
Lost River Ranger District: 588–2224
Sawtooth National Recreation Area: 726–7672
Stanley Ranger District: 774–3681
Yankee Fork Ranger District: 838–2201
Emergency: 911

Useful Local Area Web Sites

Salmon-Challis National Forest: www.fs.fed.us/r4/sc
Sawtooth National Recreation Area: www.fs.fed.us/r4/sawtooth
Sun Valley Area Reservations: www.inidaho.com
Sun Valley Area Reservations: www.sun-valley-idaho.com
Sun Valley Guide Online: www.sunvalleycentral.com
Sun Valley Resort Information: www.sunvalley.com
USDA Forest Service: www.fs.fed.us

More Web Sites of Interest

Cycling around the clock: www.cycling.tv
Cycling News: www.cyclingnews.com
DirtWorld: www.dirtworld.com/trails
Idaho BLM: www.id.blm.gov
Idaho Conservation League: www.wildidaho.org
Idaho Sierra Club: www.sierraclub.org/id
Idaho State Parks: www.idahoparks.org
Idaho Web site: www.visitidaho.org
International Mountain Biking Association: www.imba.com
Pocatello Mountain Biking: www.isu.edu/outdoor/mtbike.htm
Tour de France: www.letour.fr
Trails around the US: www.trails.com

The Author's Story (embellished version)

This is the part where I get to spew something ridiculous about myself to you, my captive audience, who is either driving to a trailhead right now and you just happened upon this page, or else you're sitting on the toilet. Don't read too long there, you'll get roids!

So here we go . . . Greg and Darla McBob (family nickname) are both born and raised Idahoans. They have been enjoying the Wood River and Sawtooth Valleys since they were born and continue to actively pursue their dreams locally. (Those dreams would also include things like trailside yoga, peak-meditation, margarita-chanting at sundown, and climbing the walls of the house, as you'll never really know what we mean there . . .)

When not writing, Greg and Darla enjoy a good bike ride.

As a little girl, Darla used to be bathed in the local hot springs around Stanley by her parents, who built many of the roads around central Idaho. Today she bathes occasionally, but still enjoys the hot springs. Greg, on the other hand, grew up mostly in Pocatello (the other windy city), but spent every waking moment he could at the old family cabin out Eagle Creek north of Ketchum. (The fact that it's still standing amazes everyone who has ever partied there.)

Greg and Darla met in Ketchum, became best friends, got married, and are currently raising their little girl, Quinn. (Or maybe it's the other way around, we're still not sure. If you have kids, you know what we're talking about.)

Today the McBobs enjoy composing symphonic music, writing plays, singing opera, and creating new rhythm dances with the neighborhood dogs. Darla is pursuing a business in interior redesign with a flair for creating unique wall colorations. Greg, on the other hand, is currently getting his doctorate in Sales Rep Stress Management, with an emphasis in Humanis Hangis Fromwallis, a relatively new field in business play management.

Greg McBobbie (as he is called in New Zealand) started writing this guidebook originally back in 1995, and after three years of research on all of the trails, he compiled the information and created the first *Good Dirt Mountain Bike Guide* in 1998. Greg wrote the original *Good Dirt* in response to getting ticked off at the other area guidebooks for inaccurate information. Sad, but true. The first ride documented was Fox Peak.

If you're a guidebook author, you understand that this is a passion, with the only reward being solely personal and not financial. Please enjoy this book, and love it as much as I have in creating it for you.